Adv

"With the recent increase in burn[...]
vides us with a timely and welcon[...]
avoiding burnout are clear and practical. I particularly like his insistence on prioritizing self-care, as health care workers often feel that they have to put themselves last. The book will also help readers deal with their own traumas—within themselves, their families, and workplaces that have become toxic."

—**David M. Allen, M.D.**, Professor of Psychiatry Emeritus, University of Tennessee Health Science Center, author of *Coping with Critical, Demanding, and Dysfunctional Parents; How Dysfunctional Families Spur Mental Disorders;* coeditor of *Groupthink in Science*

"Reading this wise and brilliant book is a crucial act of radical compassion for self and other. The tone and content are a kind of soothing balm that inspires all exhausted, brilliant, worn out, beautiful, and frazzled caregivers to slow down, become intentional, and make space to heal themselves so that they can do so more effectively with those they serve."

—**Doreen Dodgen-Magee, Psy.D.**, Psychologist, author of *Restart: Designing a Healthy Post-Pandemic Life*

"Dr. Reda has managed to pen a powerfully vulnerable, beautiful, complete call to action for the quintessential healer. *The Wounded Healer* serves as a reminder that healers/caretakers are most effective in facilitating the healing of others when they, too, are tending to their healing. In this book you will experience how individuals learned to share their pain through stories; the profound healing power of love; a focus on self-compassion and self-care as a means of meaningful existence; the significance of connection and healthy attachments to heal; and the reality that trauma does not happen in a vacuum. Dr. Reda leaves the reader with this great hope and truth: the wounded healer can and deserves to also be healed."

—**Alisha Moreland-Capuia, M.D.**, author of *Training for Change: Transforming Systems to be Trauma-Informed, Culturally Responsive and Neuroscientifically Focused* and *The Trauma of Racism: Exploring the Systems and People Fear Built*

The
Wounded
Healer

The
Wounded
Healer

THE PAIN AND JOY OF CAREGIVING

OMAR REDA, M.D.

FOREWORD BY RICHARD F. MOLLICA
AFTERWORD BY EDWARD M. SMINK

W. W. NORTON & COMPANY
Independent Publishers Since 1923

Important Note: THE WOUNDED HEALER is intended to provide general information on the subject of health and well-being; it is not a substitute for medical or psychological treatment and may not be relied upon for purposes of diagnosing or treating any illness. Please seek out the care of a professional healthcare provider if you are pregnant, nursing, or experiencing symptoms of any potentially serious condition.

For information about permission to reproduce selections from this book, write to Permissions, W. W. Norton & Company, Inc., 500 Fifth Avenue, New York, NY 10110

For information about special discounts for bulk purchases, please contact W. W. Norton Special Sales at specialsales@wwnorton.com or 800-233-4830

Manufacturing by Versa Press
Production manager: Katelyn MacKenzie

ISBN: 978-1-324-01923-7 (pbk.)

W. W. Norton & Company, Inc., 500 Fifth Avenue, New York, N.Y. 10110
www.wwnorton.com

W. W. Norton & Company Ltd., 15 Carlisle Street, London W1D 3BS

1 2 3 4 5 6 7 8 9 0

To those risking their safety and sacrificing their comfort, so we can enjoy ours.

To our heroes, the caregivers on the frontlines of suffering, engaged in sacred acts of healing.

You are loved, valued, and appreciated.

Remember to nurse your wounds and tend to your souls.

Stay with the pain.
The wound is the place where the light enters you.

—RUMI

Contents

Author's Note

In mental hospitals, it is not the sick you find, but their victims

I am acutely aware that humans have the power and the ability to cause the most damage to each other, and also the most healing.

I feel that it is my duty to tell my story and share insights gained along the journey of tending to my wounds. And even though nothing in my story was planned, my choice was what to do with all the pain weighing heavily on my heart.

For me, trauma is a source of passion and a driving force to be of service. I proudly wear it as a badge of honor. I share openly not only myself, but also my family and the people and events that inspired and transformed me, hoping to be a source of light and inspiration for you to look after your needs and console your soul. Part of being an effective caregiver is to leave some gas in your tank for tomorrow's journey.

My focus on family, faith, gratitude, and service are foundations that anchor me. To read my author biography, go through the pages of *The Wounded Healer*.

Acknowledgments

I am deeply humbled. It is such a blessing to be able to write about a topic that is very near and dear to my heart. I am grateful for the opportunity, and I hope and pray this book will serve as a tool for empowering and healing millions of wounded healers worldwide.

I want to express appreciation for my parents for instilling in me the love to serve. To my mom, my best friend and my role model, you are never gone, you are the source of light when life goes dark. And dad, proud and safe I walk in your shade.

My deepest love and gratitude for Nura, my wife and better half, for being my anchor and the driving force behind everything I do, and to my three beautiful girls, Rabha, Khadija, and Fatima, for being the joy and delight of our life.

Thank you, Professor Richard Mollica, for teaching me that there is no healing without the search for beauty; and Dr. Edward Smink, for believing in me and being a guide and mentor on this sacred path. There are no words to express how blessed and lucky I am to have both of you in my life. Your words of wisdom echo throughout this journey, and your kind souls have helped me craft a book with a soul.

Much gratitude to Deborah Malmud, Mariah Eppes, Sara McBride

Tuohy, Olivia Guarnieri, Kelly Auricchio, Emma Paolini, Megan Bedell, Kevin Olsen, and the whole editorial and marketing team at Norton for the opportunity to turn this dream into reality, and to Patricia Watson and Sarah Johnson for their impressive editorial and technical assistance, making the book concise, organized, and easy to navigate, despite its emotionally heavy content.

None of this would have been possible without the support of my coworkers, the stories of my clients, and mainly the sacrifices of my colleagues, the frontline staff. I admire your courage; you are my heroes. You are loved, valued, and appreciated. It is an extreme honor to write about you.

Foreword

The most skillful physicians are those who, from their youth upwards, have combined with the knowledge of their art the greatest experience of disease; ...and should have had all manner of diseases in their own person.

PLATO, REPUBLIC 3.408[1]

Dr. Omar Reda offers us a kind, affectionate, and gentle look at the injuries and wounds suffered by the healing professions. His deep insights emerge out of his own suffering as a Libyan psychiatrist working in the United States who has suffered personal work-related injuries in his life as well as the experience of being a displaced exile and refugee. He is a *wounded healer* whose inner "woundedness" has transformed his own pain, vulnerability, and suffering to his capacity to empathize with and serve directly his "wounded" health care colleagues. Dr. Reda leads us on a hopeful and inspiring journey of healing and recovery. His great love and appreciation of his fellow health workers is evident. He provides his colleagues not only a road map to repair their professional trauma, but also a pathway to wellness and flourishing.

In our work at the Harvard Program in Refugee Trauma with highly traumatized refugees and communities over the past four decades, it has become obvious that no one is immune to tragic life experiences over a lifetime. Tragedy occurs to everyone; and out of this tragedy emerges a solidarity between doctor/healer and patient/client. In the many stories offered in this book, Dr. Reda illustrates the power of this solidarity as he forges a relationship between the health care worker's inner self, the patient, and the medical system. He clearly answers to that inner voice that empathically and quietly declares, "I know that you know that I know" the pain and suffering you are experiencing. Dr. Reda loves to speak about the boundaries that are broken and that cause illness; his empathic vision also restores the boundaries that heal.

Dr. Reda's work follows in a special tradition in Western medicine: the concept of the *wounded healer*. This concept or belief in the healing power of the transformation of a healer's woundedness began with Plato and emerged out of ancient Greek medicine centered upon the god of medical healing, *Asclepios* (Aesculapius). The concept of the *wounded healer* flourished and was noted across cultures, having its earliest roots in shamanistic communities and religious healing practices of the Italian Renaissance. It was not until the mid-twentieth century that it was named and codified in writings by the great psychoanalyst, Carl Jung, and the modern pastoral counselors such as Henri Nouwen. The term *wounded healer* is now commonly used in peer counseling, self-help groups, and Alcoholics Anonymous.

Dr. Reda's perspective, however, is special and unique. This book is original insofar as it gives voice to the concept of the *wounded healer* by a non-Western, middle Eastern psychiatrist. This is a wonderful addition to the *wounded healer* tradition. It is crucial in our complex multicultural world that the voices of medical doctors and health practitioners from diverse backgrounds be heard and listened to with respect. The COVID-19 pandemic has revealed the enormous burden of illness placed on health care workers and community members who are persons of color. Dr. Reda is in a unique position as a bicultural health care professional who has witnessed our health care system as both an insider and an outsider. It is our belief that those who work on the margins of a system can truly see what is going on within the inner workings of the conventional mainstream institutions. Wonderfully, Dr. Reda has this penetrating gaze.

This book is written by an author who reveals systematically in his narrated stories four elements of a powerful storyteller.

Courage

Dr. Reda is extremely courageous. His personal history as a war survivor and refugee, modestly told, reveals his personal courage dealing with a traumatic past. Most importantly, he transforms this courage into speaking out against the toxicity of our medical system. As a minority physician, he has harnessed the courage to speak out against what is occurring in the medical system that is hurting his colleagues emotionally and physically. He asserts firmly his fight against structural racism and misogyny. For example, he tells a tale about a wonderful doctor being harassed by HR after making an error and not being supported by her supervisor; a painful story of a doctor committing suicide on-site at a hospital by throwing herself off a building in front of her colleagues with only "lip service" following the event as support; and the institutional neglect of dealing with an African American patient being unfairly placed in restraints. In our self-care project, www.HPRT-selfcare.org, we strongly advocate Dr. Reda's message that hypocritical institutional mission statements may, in fact, be cover-ups that hide institutional neglect, which lead to staff and patient injury. Dr. Reda is bold enough to state that if your place of work is toxic, you need to get out as soon as possible.

Apocalyptic Experience

Clearly Dr. Reda is a healer who has worked in extreme catastrophic situations. He is deeply aware from his own personal experience of extreme environments that the suffering and pain of trauma survivors is readily transmitted to their healers. Bringing his real-life learned knowledge to the United States, he finds that "burnout" and "compassion fatigue," like the PTSD experience of war trauma, are a universal experience of the healing professions. He states that the pain and suffering caused by the everyday experience of medical care is commonplace and is intensified within a toxic environment. Dr. Reda strongly advocates for the well-being of the families of the helping professional and support staff, lessons learned from war. "Top priority: take care of family and loved ones first" is his self-care mantra. It is critical, before anything else, to pay attention to the welfare of your family, including spouse, grandparents, and children, as well as to protect them from the damage that can be brought home from the hospital or clinic. Dr. Reda provides practices in real time that can aid health care workers to care for their family members.

Resonance

Dr. Reda helps us to resonate to the emotional state of the health care workers and patients presented in his book. I had tears stream down my face as I read the story of an Arab doctor who was verbally attacked by a patient during a bedside exam. This patient hated Arabs; it turned out his son was killed in Afghanistan. With extreme dignity and respect, the doctor was able to negotiate this verbal attack and arrive at a shared empathic place with the patient. Dr. Reda helps us experience this moment of "rupture and repair" along with the attending physician and patient. Without judgment, Dr. Reda was able to help us understand the life experiences of doctor and patient.

Empathy

This is a loving and affectionate book, full of empathy and hope. Dr. Reda does not hide his love for his family, but also the love and respect he has for his colleagues and patients. In beautiful stories he reveals the caring of a patient who has to die alone after being rejected by her family and a woman who lost a beloved spouse to COVID-19 without a family member present at death. Empathy, for Dr. Reda, is the ointment that heals. Of course, his love for beauty and his quote of our HPRT mantra that "there is no healing without beauty" is greatly appreciated.

Dr. Omar Reda is a *wounded healer* who out of great love for his family, his colleagues, and his patients, has written a timely book that offers us remedies for dealing with our own brokenness and woundedness. My professor at Yale, the late Dr. Stanley Jackson, who was a historian of the *wounded healer*,[2] offers us an inspiring quote that serves as a beautiful metaphor to Dr. Reda's book:

Wounded oysters build out of gory wounds a pearl.
And create within the gap of pain a jewel.
May we be so wise....
The pearl is the transformation of pain.[3]

Richard F. Mollica, M.D., MAR
Professor of Psychiatry, Harvard Medical School
Director, Harvard Program in Refugee Trauma
Massachusetts General Hospital

References

1. Plato. (1937). *The republic*, in *The dialogues of Plato*. Trans. B. Jowett. New York: Random House.
2. Jackson, S. W. (2001). The wounded healer. *Bull Hist Med*, *75*, 1–36.
3. Shannon, R. (1976). *The peacock and the phoenix: Poems, 1963–1971: Designs and Text, 1970–1975*. Millbrae, California: Celestial Arts.

Introduction

There Is Cost to Caring

Being a caregiver is a badge of honor. To be able to serve is a true privilege, a gift that is received with deep gratitude and shared through acts of service.

Caring for others can be physically exhausting and emotionally draining, yet many caregivers describe it as fulfilling and gratifying. Caregiving comes with a wide range of rewards; materialistic ones are usually at the bottom of the list of what inspire healers to join the field. Most of the benefits that come from caregiving are emotional, social, spiritual, and moral. Caregiving is a blessing, an affair of the soul, a sacred mission. But when working with traumatized individuals, families, and communities, care providers are not only prone to vicarious trauma listening to the stories of others; many healers also tend to neglect their own needs and boundaries, risking compassion fatigue and burnout. If not careful, caregivers can be traumatized by the very act of caregiving.

Prolonged exposure to human suffering is not without risks. Many caregivers score poorly on burnout and quality-of-life questionnaires. That is why it is important to remind them to tend to their souls. Caregiving done right can make caregivers beam with joy and pride. Healthy caregivers blossom when given the chance to meet their full potential. When crushed by the many dysfunctions of the system, however, they might start to second-guess their worth and struggle with self-doubt, even if their professional performance as providers of care is stellar.

When exhausted, rather than talking about their needs and proactively taking steps toward fulfilling them, they might take their fatigue and negative energy out on themselves or their loved ones. Caregiver fatigue and toxic stress take their toll on the soul, on physical and mental health, on family bonds, on social life, and on the ability to be at our best. Trauma can add multiple layers of heavy burden to an already deeply injured industry.

The concept of the wounded healer is very much an unacknowledged reality in the healthcare field. Psychosocial wounds are the elephant in the room that remains largely ignored. The problem is that pretending something does not exist will not make it go away. If we do not pay attention to the emotional impact of caregiving, we might end up spending significant amounts of time, energy, and resources dealing with the consequences.

Many factors render caregivers susceptible to caregiver fatigue, though some of the qualities that characterize caregivers can work to protect them from it. For example, their efforts to master self-awareness and self-management can make them more able to handle emotionally loaded encounters. But caregivers often have other traits that can be harmful and hinder their ability to provide safe, competent, and compassionate care to others. These include believing themselves to be invincible, feigning strength at moments of deep fragility, faking confidence during times of greatest vulnerability, denying their own needs, shutting off their feelings, and turning a blind eye to their own bleeding wounds of trauma. Caregivers may also hold detrimental attitudes that stigmatize seeking support, expressing emotions, and paying attention to the impacts of their suffering on the family unit and on other relationships.

Caregivers might feel tangled when lines are blurred. Because the relationships with the self, family, and others are intertwined, boundaries get crossed, and unfortunately, when we allow others to treat us as doormats, they learn to walk all over us. Sometimes we will be the ones who seem to be inviting such dysfunction, when we do not respect our own boundaries. I know many colleagues who are reluctant to say "no" even when they are totally depleted, but the truth is people will respect you more when you show self-respect through asserting healthy boundaries. It is okay to say "no" to one task so you are more able to authentically show up and say an enthusiastic "yes" to another. Part of protecting your sanity is respecting your boundaries. When it comes to suffering in isolation, some caregivers refuse to reach out for help because of attitudes like "I can do it on my own" or "I do not want to be a burden," stances that are counterproductive and not conducive to self-healing.

There are unique challenges facing caregivers. A central challenge is a deep-seated stigma about emotional expression, which, when coupled with a sense of obligation to protect those they care for, can be a perfect recipe for a toxic environment of silent suffering caregivers find themselves in. Many caregivers believe that their feelings do not matter, and that they should ignore their needs, deny their pain, brush off their trauma, wipe away their tears, and just "suck it up" and keep going. In this book, I intend to keep it real by digging deep, going behind the fake smiles, exposing a culture of secrecy, toxic stress, and silent suffering. I can no longer accept being a passive bystander or bearing false witness while so many of my colleagues and coworkers are getting crushed under the wheels of systems that are broken and know no mercy. Caregivers are the most valuable assets in the healthcare industry. They need to know that and believe in their infinite worth. They do that when they value their contribution and honor their own voice through leaning in and practicing self-compassion.

Self-care is neither an elusive goal nor an empty promise that is preached but not practiced, and it should never be viewed as a luxury or be a source of guilt or shame. Rather, self-care is a responsibility that must be taken seriously, and a commitment that needs to be fulfilled if caregivers are to be expected to continue to give care. Caregivers who take care of their needs find more joy caring for others and are better able to continue to show up to serve.

My Reasons for Writing This Book

I am deeply humbled by the generous amount of love and support I received from caring colleagues; it enabled me to be who and where I am today, and for that I am forever grateful. To express my gratitude, I intend to show up with compassion for others at their time of need and to be with trauma survivors on the frontlines of their suffering.

I have encountered multiple forms of trauma myself, like losing loved ones to terrorism and violent extremism; going through the journey of forced migration, asylum-seeking, and living in exile; and coming face-to-face with the dark side of humanity. I had the option either to become part of the problem, repeating the dysfunction and getting tangled in a deadly web of retraumatization, or to choose instead to get untangled, become part of the solution, and break the cycle of trauma. The choice was clear. With grace illuminating my soul and faith strengthening my resolve, I saw my experiences as a privilege that humbles and disciplines me, and I viewed my trauma story as a calling to serve and as a tool to help others heal.

Trauma is Greek for wound. Wounded does not equal broken. To get traumatized is neither a character flaw, nor a moral failure, or sign of weakness. Trauma does not have to permanently damage or paralyze us. In fact, trauma can be the source of our growth and transformation. The main message of this book is simple: caregivers are stronger and more resilient because of their trauma. We need to share our stories and make meaning out of suffering.

The *Encyclopedia of Trauma* (Figley, 2012) describes trauma as a penetration that ranges in severity from minor to lethal, one that leaves scars and vulnerability. Large-scale trauma like natural disasters can cause major disruptions to multiple ecological systems, yet it is interpersonal violence and human brutality that tends to deeply injure the psyche and wound the soul of its survivor. This is true for the clients we serve, and it is true for us as wounded healers.

ACCORDING TO THE *ENCYCLOPEDIA OF TRAUMA* (FIGLEY, 2012):

Trauma attacks the soul. After its first three effects: the initial impact, exhaustion, and grief, the fourth and most crucial impact of traumatic stress is on the soul. Belief injuries can permanently disrupt assumptions of love, kindness, forgiveness, morality, values, principles, identity, convictions, ideals, religion, meaning, and purpose. Burnout unfolds from repeated traumatic assaults on the psyche.

Yes, repeated attacks on the soul can cause major ruptures and disruptions, yet we can help prevent permanent damage if we learn how to self-attune to console our souls.

Trauma is intrinsic to the healthcare profession. Medicine is sometimes described as the field of suffering. Caregivers bear witness to the most intimate and graphic details of inflicted pain and violated trust. If not paying close attention to the impact of caregiving on themselves, healthcare workers can risk paying a very heavy price for caring for others.

One major goal of this book is to expose the culture of secrecy surrounding the field of caregiving. As a first step to caring for ourselves as healers and frontline staff, we need to actively combat stigma through humanizing caregiving and normalizing self-care. We do that when we tackle topics like taboo, shame, and guilt; the sense of obligation; the illusion of invincibility; and the superhuman mentality.

Alleviating caregivers' suffering is an especially important communal responsibility of the healthcare industry. As a fellow wounded healer, I am humbly inviting all of you to pay attention to your internal processes and to appreciate not only the rewards that come through caregiving—the lives saved, the loved ones comforted, the wounds healed, and the hearts mended—but also to show appreciation for the sacrifices of those on the frontlines. Let us not take them for granted. Even machines deserve breaks. I have seen colleagues quit the field they once loved, engage in risky and dangerous behaviors to numb the pain of their moral injuries, and, unfortunately, find no other way out of hopelessness and despair than by self-destruction or ending their lives.

We must find ways to fill our emotional tanks and fulfill our unmet needs if we are to continue to care for others. If we always give and never receive, there will come a time when there is nothing left in us to give. When one of my colleagues takes their own life or uses self-destructive and unhealthy ways to cope with the stress of caregiving, it is a stain of shame on our collective conscience.

Provider burnout is preventable, but the fight against it requires all of us. We need to change the culture of denial and start watching out for and supporting one another.

Trauma can lead to wisdom and enlightenment, not only to pain and suffering. My trauma motivated me to become a healer and was the source of inspiration to write this book. To put things into perspective, I am going to tell caregivers' stories, including mine, focusing on encounters that ignited in us the desire and passion to serve.

We are all caregivers in one way or another: parents as their children grow up, children when their parents get older, family members of those with physical and mental disabilities, teachers, community and religious leaders, law enforcement officers, first responders, and the many more invisible heroes on the frontlines serving as the glue that holds their families and communities together. We wear multiple hats and serve in different capacities and contexts. The stress of one identity might exacerbate or get exacerbated by others. All caregivers are to be honored and celebrated. The tips, tools, and skills discussed here will likely be helpful to all caregivers, regardless of their professional background, but the focus of this work is on caregivers in the healthcare system.

My own experiences will inform this writing, as they do my clinical work. The book aims to aid providers in their self-care and help them accelerate their own healing by bearing witness to the challenges facing them, and by suggesting tools and strategies they can use to help themselves heal and, in doing so, help them provide better care for their clients and their loved ones.

The stories I will tell here are composites that I feel will help illustrate some of the common stressors caregivers experience. Following the journeys of six fictional characters and my own true story will hopefully cover intimate and sacred encounters that caregivers engage in every day. Stories of loss, trauma, despair, and pain, but more importantly stories of resilience, healing, beauty, and joy.

Bearing Witness to Stories of Caregivers

I would have loved the opportunity to sit down to interview every single caregiver to celebrate their experiences and honor their voices, but millions of stories are unlikely to fit into this one book.

Over the past several months, I interviewed many of my coworkers in different contexts and formats. I sat with diverse staff in various units, both individually and in groups and team settings. The colleagues I talked to while working on this project have attempted to answer my question, "What would you want to see in a book that is written about you?" What I heard was that many of us are tangled in a web of challenges in our homes, in our places of work, and in our communities. I will not be able to cover everything, but I will try my best to touch on common themes. I hope you will be able to identify with some or all of the characters in the book. You are valuable, and this platform is intended to value you through honoring your voice and validating your experiences.

While embarking on this exciting journey, I had the great pleasure and privilege of bearing witness to stories of many healers. I asked individual staff members and teams of healers questions like:

- Do you feel that your life has a clear purpose?
- Do you feel optimistic about your future?
- Do you feel that what you do is valuable?
- Do you feel that people appreciate you as a person?

I also asked open-ended questions to help facilitate speaking up—about feeling drained, in particular, and also about burnout, self-care, and help-seeking. Those questions included:

- Why did you choose to become a caregiver? What was your inspiration?

- How has caregiving impacted your physical health?
- How has caregiving impacted your mental health?
- How has caregiving impacted your spiritual health?
- How has caregiving impacted your family dynamics?
- How has caregiving impacted your social life?
- What are some ways that you have tried to cope with the stress of caregiving?
- What do you do to take care of yourself?
- Why do you still continue to be a caregiver despite the price you are paying for caring for others?
- Do you talk to others about the impact of caregiving on you?

I invite you, too, if you feel comfortable doing so, to honestly answer these questions. Share difficult feelings with your support system and with your loved ones, and if needed, reach out for professional help. Speaking up is a sign of courage, not weakness.

I will be sharing tons of resources I have collected over the years, drawing from the wisdom of many respected pioneers in our field of humane and compassionate care. Throughout the pages of the book, you will get to meet them and hear their voices. The most important voice that needs to be heard, however, is yours.

All stories are important. Covering the stress of caregiving while homeschooling, parenting, or taking care of elderly parents and loved ones, or while being active within or outside one's own community, though important, is beyond the scope of this project. I will touch briefly on this theme, but by no means can I do it justice.

The message I want you to hear is that I see you, I hear you, I feel you, and I want you to know that, as a caregiver, but most importantly as a human, you are loved and treasured. Do not feel that you are alone, and never fall into despair. I want you to know that you are valuable, what you do matters, and who you are matters more. When life becomes too hard and things start to get out of control, remember that you have people who care about you, reach out to them and allow them to reach in to hold you.

When I was approached to write this book, I told the publishing team that I wanted to write a book with a soul. You, caregivers, are the soul of this book. Being a wounded healer is a miracle of grace.

My Promise to Readers

This is a book about the joy and delight, not the pain and burden, of caregiving. It is not a message of despair. On the contrary, it is full of hope and it invites you to find beauty amid suffering.

It is not a book about provider burnout, vicarious trauma, or compassion fatigue. These topics are extremely important and quite relevant to the field of caregiving, and I am pleased that there has been extensive focus on helping healers navigate through them. I will expand instead on the intra- and inter-personal challenges that care providers face, both inside and outside their places of healing. I am going that route because caregiving is not only an act we perform in our places of employment, but also, for many of us, is a lifestyle that extends to all aspects of our lives as healers and also as parents, children, spouses, siblings, neighbors, members of society, and brothers and sisters in humanity.

I will share not only my expertise but also my passion. I poured my heart and soul into this book. The writing comes from the very bottom of my heart, and I hope it touches yours. I will examine the humanity of the therapeutic relationship. We do amazing work saving lives and transforming them in physical and nonphysical ways. I intend to shed a particularly bright light on the plight of traumatized caregivers, also known as wounded healers. The book explores the unique joys and challenges facing caregivers and extends an invitation for them to nurse their wounds while helping others. Caregivers might share experiences similar to those of the people they care for, and mutual healing can therefore happen, especially in times of crisis, but really always, by using tools such as gratitude and service and by practicing self-compassion.

There is hope despite trauma. I am a strong believer in the ability of the human spirit to not only survive but also thrive when tested with adversity. I would even argue that it is not despite the trauma, but because of it, that people experience growth, resiliency, and beauty.

This book was written during a global pandemic. The COVID-19 crisis exposed a heavily wounded and deeply divided America, and similar trends could be seen in many parts of the world. There has been a sharp increase in the rates of anxiety, fear, depression, despair, anger, hate, grief, alcohol and drug use, family discord, child abuse, domestic violence, and suicidal thoughts and behaviors. I have seen this in my patients and have felt a significant amount of restless energy within my small community, the general public, throughout the nation and the whole world. In the book, I go over my observations of the visible and invisible effects of the coronavirus, and its psychosocial impacts. I am sounding the alarm not to scare, rather to prepare. And while the issues in this book existed long before the pandemic, and will continue long after it, the current and near-future moment urgently brings them forward.

In this world, there will always be pain and trauma, but there will also always be people who are willing to show up for others. We have seen beautiful examples of solidarity, random acts of kindness, and encounters of deep humanity during the pandemic, and I hope we build on that through focusing on the beauty of the human spirit.

I am trying to leave a legacy through sharing stories that humanize my caregiver colleagues and give them platforms and safe spaces so they can regain their voice and reclaim their narrative. No one deserves to lose their voice, to suffer in silence, to live in the shadows, or to feel alone or desperate in a world that is filled with people and abundant resources. When we lose one of our caregivers, we all lose.

I have learned so much along the journey of overcoming my trauma. I share this wisdom with you here to help facilitate speaking up on behalf of those who are otherwise forgotten, voiceless, and feeling alone and alienated, suffering in silence behind closed doors. I want to honor survivors of trauma and open a sacred holding space in my heart for their stories, and also to bear witness and renew a commitment to not repeating the cycle or being part of the problem.

My intention in sharing parts of my story is to encourage you to practice self-compassion so that you, too, may tell your story, nurse your wounds, and get more comfortable hugging yourself.

It is my genuine desire and my sincere intention to share a message of hope with you. We can find the joy of caregiving when we break free from the cycles of secrecy, toxic stress, and silent suffering. I hope you leave this book feeling empowered and inspired, so you may continue to empower and inspire those you care for.

Go through this journey any way you see fit. Given the potential emotional impact of bearing witness to the stories narrated in this book, I have provided a space for reflection and introspection after each chapter. Please pause if you feel the need to do so and look with compassion after your needs. This book is intended to be a healing tool, for you to nurse your wounds and to tend to your soul.

It is now my absolute pleasure to invite you to join me on a journey to meet and honor you, *The Wounded Healer.*

The
Wounded
Healer

1 / Bearing Witness: The Pain and Joy of Interacting With Clients

The Heart of Caregiving

Survivors of compassion fatigue and the darkness of burnout remind us that caregiving is not only at the core of being human, it *is* the core of being human. Caregivers bear witness to the human experience, from birth to death, with all its laughter and tears, its trials and tribulations. That is what being human is all about, the humanity and the being.

Patients come to the attention of caregivers not because they are broken, but, often, because of a relational rupture. Caregivers then repair, rather than fix, that existential damage through the simple yet profound act of deep kindness and being-with.

Caring acts can bring joy to caring souls. Entering the landscape of pain, according to Dr. Edward Smink (2018), is a heroic act, even though caregivers do not see themselves as heroes. To console, hold, and sustain others while they are "falling apart" requires heroic skills. Yet that can be a heavy burden, so make sure you tend to your soul.

Be gentle and embrace self-compassion. I often hear from colleagues that their souls ache, and I feel it sometimes myself. Human suffering can suck the life and joy out of us. That is why we need to frequently pause to reflect and find safe and healthy ways to recharge and recenter so we can become better able to engage with the people we serve.

Caring for Others Necessitates Self-Care

Caring for others without taking breaks to care for ourselves is irrational. We understand that logic in our head, but we seem to not be able to register it in our heart. We engage constantly in a struggle between our sense of obligation when we bear witness to the suffering of others, and between the loud and clear screams of our inner voice begging us to pause and reflect. Yet caregivers, for the most part, neglect their own needs when engaged in caring acts. Why do we keep doing that? We will examine throughout the book themes that keep us stuck, alone, and not knowing where to turn, being slaves to a world that sucks us dry and then gets angry at us when we are depleted. Not to mention the existence of systemic issues, some of those, like discrimination, harassment, intimidation, and threats of retaliation, are too serious to be tolerated or ignored. I tend to quickly leave toxic environments that tolerate or condone staff abuse. I have the luxury of being able to do so, given my status as a psychiatrist, but I have witnessed with heartbreak countless crushed souls, staff who are stuck in dysfunctional systems because they have obligations, children to feed and families to take care of. It is a shame when caregivers stay at a job they dread for fear of losing their family's source of income.

Self-awareness is critical. We caregivers bear witness to the stories of our clients, but we should not neglect our own. In the process of honoring their voices, we find ours. It is extremely important to assert healthy boundaries when nursing the wounds of others. Part of being trauma informed is being self-aware.

In his profoundly beautiful and powerful book, *The Soul of Caregiving*, Edward Smink (2018) extends a generous invitation for us to dive deep into the soul of being a healer. Smink sees caregiving as an act of love and a spiritual practice. He argues that "compassion resilience is a byproduct of compassion fatigue." He refers to our reactions to trauma as "shadows" and invites us, when we are depleted, to notice them and embrace them with compassion: "When you meet a shadow, practice forgiveness," he urges.

Smink (2018) refers to the sense of dread, emotional exhaustion, and spiritual draining that we feel as a "soul ache." He reminds us of the beauty within each of us. I see that beauty every day, working with dedicated colleagues committed to bringing healing and determined to make the world a better place. I believe, however, that the world will become even better if basic needs of caregivers are fulfilled. "You cannot give what you have not discovered," Smink (2018) reminds us; we must periodically reflect on our spiritual calling as caregivers. "Because caregiving is an act of love, it is not for the faint of heart, or the hard of heart, or even the half-hearted. It is a path to self-knowledge and finding one's soul."

Working with the wounded, the afflicted, the diseased, and the dying enriches our soul's stamina, quality, and resilience. "Fatigue flattens compassion," he warns, and our scars are an invitation to rediscover our soul.

Smink (2018) beautifully adds that

> We reach the hearts of others and touch their souls through caregiving. Each encounter with our clients and our own souls has the potential to become an opportunity to get transformed. Soul

is the animated spirit that inspires how we do what we do. It is from the soul that we find the energy that sustains us. Caregiving requires serious soul-searching. A soulful action is not only reserved for mystics, monks, or hermits. Activities of the soul are found at the heart of being human. Reach in and reach out. The very essence of the soul is to be in a relationship. We meet the sacred in others and discover it in ourselves.

This is incredibly insightful. People will not care how much you know until they know how much you care. The more we care, the more deeply we impact and get impacted by the dynamics of our relationships with the people we care for.

That is why I made the conscious decision to actively search for beauty every time I meet with a client. Here is one recent encounter that ended up much better than I expected. I believe that, without a compassionate search for sacred beauty, the outcome would likely have been quite different.

My new patient: Oh, Reda, not Rita? Well, that's a funny name. Where are you from?
 Me: Originally? North Africa.

Patient: Well, I don't like you.
 Me: Why's that?

Patient: That whole continent should just drown. You're nothing but gangsters and criminals.
 Me: Wow, you've some strong feelings about people of color. Did something happen?

Patient (now crying): A bunch of thugs hit my father on the head, an armed robbery. His brain bled to death.

Me: I'm so sorry for your loss. [pause] And thank you for sharing that painful memory with me. How would you like us to proceed with our relationship?

Patient: I know that I sound like a racist, and I know that not all of you are bad.

I was happy with what transpired in that first session. She felt safe enough to share parts of her trauma story, and I was there to bear witness to it. Her deeply hurtful words were coming from a place of her own deep hurt.

I worked next on channeling that angry energy so she could use her grief in a healthy way and be better able to honor the memory of her loved one and celebrate his legacy. It was an act of kindness that cost me nothing but likely spared both of us lots of heartache.

A Journey of the Heart

Smink (2018) reminds us that caregiving is done best if we host with our hearts.

> Caregivers are hosts, they treat their guests with hospitality, sharing the best of what they have. Hospitality entertains curiosity about the guest's story without neglecting that of the host. Welcome the interior movements of your soul. At the heart of compassion is hospitality. As you welcome the stranger, your own humanity and dignity get restored. To care for a guest is to welcome the divine.

Some cultures believe that if you drink a first cup of tea you are a guest, if you enjoy a second cup you are a friend, and if you share the third you become family. Caregivers can bring these beautiful dynamics to light when they share intimate moments with their clients, offering their hearts to people at times of both distress and delight.

But we can lose that connection if we lose sight of our true calling. "You are only human if you have a heart. To disconnect from heart and service invites shadows," Smink (2018) declares.

> Caregiving is divine. Caregiving is who we are. But when the shadows take over, a caregiver becomes a caretaker, the well of caregiving within starts to run dry. When you lose the soul of your calling, it becomes just a job, a paycheck, a burden, no longer a joy. It is one thing to see caregiving as a job, and it is totally a different thing to see it as a calling.

Burnout can lead to soul ache. Lack of self-care can make us lose our moral compass and take dangerous detours. Bad personal and professional outcomes can then happen. Medical errors, accidents, impaired work habits, mental and emotional difficulties—these can all take place because we are traumatized. Our trauma can be related or not related to the workplace. There is a cost to caring. There is a price to be paid for being a caregiver. Hence the importance of restorative activities, honest and serious soul-searching, and a renewed, constant, and consistent commitment to self-care.

Caregiver stressors

Caregivers face many challenges, inside and outside their places of employment. Those include personal and family stressors, workplace dynamics, and "bigger picture" systemic issues they find themselves tangled in. For healers to heal, they need to sort through multiple and complex layers of trauma. The first step to do that is to realize these impacts and prioritize self-care.

Dr. Charles Figley (1995), in his book *Compassion Fatigue*, eloquently writes, "There is a cost to caring. Professionals who listen to clients' stories of fear, pain, and suffering may feel similar fears, pains, and sufferings because they care."

According to Smink (2018):

> Three social, cultural, and professional taboos exist that caregivers wrestle with when developing skills of self-care. The first is trust. The stories of caregivers are epic and fashion each of their lives, yet who is there to listen to their joys and struggles? Who is there to hold what seems unholdable, so the caregiver feels heard? Who has the time? And sadly, who really cares? Trusting a teammate or a supervisor may be dangerous, especially when compassion fatigue is mistakenly considered a mental illness or a sign of fragility. I have seen colleagues hide their suffering for too long because they believe that speaking up can cost them their job or pose a threat to their professional license.

Smink (2018) adds,

> The second dysfunction of our culture has to do with talking. Caregivers somehow have swallowed the code of silence hook, line, and sinker. This is seen commonly in rigid and dismissive work environments where caregivers do not speak up because, what is the point? Nothing will ever change.

Smink (2018) continues his reflections:

> Trusting colleagues can help break the cycle of silence. Caregivers have stories to tell. Stories that affect all aspects of their lives. Caregivers experience normal reactions to abnormal traumatic events. If they talk about their experiences, it affects their entire team. Each team member then becomes directly or indirectly involved. Processing a traumatic event is not a sign of weakness, but rather a sign of strength. However, we live in a culture that sees that as belonging to the "Crybabies Club."

Unprocessed traumatic memories tend to keep people stuck. Humans are programmed to try to make sense of suffering. When denied that opportunity, it confuses the psyche and adds to the soul ache.

According to Smink (2018),

> Finally, the third social taboo is about showing emotions. Who of us has been rewarded or encouraged growing up to express our feelings? How about the adage "Children are to be seen and not heard" or "Big boys do not cry"? So, we stuff our feelings and keep a stiff upper lip because we must leave our emotions in check.

Caregivers who are tangled in these dysfunctions become like robots, constantly denying their feelings, or experiencing them without the "permission" to have healthy ways to express them. I am guilty of that too. Sometimes, particularly after a rough day listening to stories of deep pain, I space out and become less emotionally available to be with my loved ones. I am working on improving that through self-awareness and being more receptive to feedback.

Cultures of Care

Workplace culture, according to Smink (2018), can break these taboos. "Trusting, talking, and expressing feelings are the antidotes in coping with compassion fatigue, in building compassion resilience, and in gaining safe and healthy tools and skills that promote self-care and restore wellness." Teams that condone silent suffering seem to struggle with dysfunctional dynamics, while teams that invest in staff well-being and watch out for one another's emotional needs are the ones that seem to thrive.

To nourish our cultures of care, Smink (2018) asks that we listen, not to give answers but to create space. The team can serve as the medium that contains suffering and promotes healing. When I attune to my teammates and they pay close attention to me, we become more aware of subtle changes in mood, demeanor, and behavior, and that in turn helps improve morale and perhaps even save lives. Noticing people revives them.

Do to colleagues as you do to clients: check in. Smink (2018) asks caregivers to work on the deep-seated stigma prevalent in the field; "You are not going mad because your soul aches." Who hugs the hugger? How are we expected to stand firm holding the unbearable if our own foundation is shaky?" Stories of caregivers, he argues, are screaming to be heard, so always be the first to check on others. A small gesture of kindness can brighten someone's dark day; be a source of light. Make sure the reaching out is mutual. Care is a two-way street. Give through service and receive with gratitude.

I have found it helpful to extend grace, such as sending an email to express appreciation for the hard work of a colleague, or telling them that face-to-face, praising them in public. That might lighten their burden and uplift their spirits. I wish leaders would do that more often. We are usually called into administrative offices only when there is "an issue."

"Moments of reprieve create time and space for us to recall, rediscover, and renew our individual call to become caregivers," argues Smink (2018). We can make space for others through engaging in acts of deep kindness. The more the better.

Despite the pain, try to focus on the joy. That is another tool that can help healers heal. I believe that with active investment in healing and beauty, we can emerge from our traumatic experiences as better versions of ourselves. It is an easy task discovering the beauty around us, but realizing our own beauty takes deep and honest self-inventory, vulnerability, and courage.

As Smink (2018) says, being a caregiver is to engage in a journey of the heart. The caregiver's guide is internal, for this journey is a pilgrimage toward one's soul, an endeavor that requires discipline of the heart. Caregiving is a divine affair, one that disciplines the heart to hold a sacred space for injured souls and gives healers the power to mend broken hearts.

The following encounter brings many of these dynamics to light. It is a story of how caregivers seem to always, somehow, manage to find holding spaces in their hearts for the suffering of others.

Hurt People Hurt People

"Okay, let's see what the day brings," said the ever-energetic Brad, a 32-year-old white physical therapist, as he joined the medicine team's clinical rounds at the hospital.

"I can't work with that Arab student," announced Mr. Sinclair snarkily from his bed, where he was recovering from a minor heart attack.

"Excuse me, what did you just say?" asked Dr. Johnson, the

attending physician, irritated, biting his tongue, and carefully thinking through his next move.

Angry and determined, the words came rushing out of the patient's mouth as if he had been holding on to them for years. "You heard me right. Those Muslims think they can just come here and take over our country. Do you see how she's dressed? This is America. Why doesn't she dress like an American or go the hell back to whatever country she came from?"

Agitated, Dr. Johnson responded, "Well, Mr. Sinclair, Dr. Salam is a resident physician, not a student, and I want to make it very clear that she's an important and valued member of this team. If you continue to choose hate and talk bad about my staff, I'm afraid I'll need to ask you to seek care somewhere else."

"Oh, Dr. Johnson, please allow me," interjected Dr. Salam, a well-liked and soft-spoken Syrian American resident physician, now shaken but trying to keep her cool. She approached the disgruntled man and calmly said, "Mr. Sinclair, would you be so kind as to please tell me what about me is making you uncomfortable? I strive to provide the best care for all of my patients. How may I put your concerns at ease?"

"Here we go with that sweet tongue of yours. I'm sure you'll say next that not all Muslims are terrorists. Well, tell that to my son who your people killed in Afghanistan." He turned his face away to hide his tears.

"Oh, Mr. Sinclair, I'm terribly sorry. I wasn't aware of such tragedy. I can only imagine how horrible it must be to lose a child," said Dr. Salam, who looked genuinely saddened by the sudden revelation.

"Oh, no, you can never imagine. Why did you kill Jimmy?"

responded Mr. Sinclair, now in a more agitated tone. "He was the sweetest boy you'll ever meet. He went to Afghanistan to help fight terrorists and help build that stupid country."

"Jimmy sounds like such a wonderful soul, Mr. Sinclair," said Dr. Salam, while offering her patient a deep look of concern. "Terrorism is ugly, and nothing excuses violence. Terrorists disguise their dark agendas and twisted ideologies under the name of religion to create animosity and hate between us. But I have nothing in common with those thugs. I left Syria running away from terrorism. I lost family members to the same monster that killed Jimmy." Visibly upset now, she added, "And I know this isn't about me. I just wanted you to know that we have more in common than what divides us."

"Mr. Sinclair, I feel your pain," exclaimed Dr. Johnson. "I was a military physician myself, and have lost many friends to war. I want to assure you, though, that people like Dr. Salam pose no threat to you or me. We're a better team because she's one of us. I wonder if you can celebrate Jimmy's memory by channeling your anger in a more healthy and productive way."

"Dr. Johnson, I died the day Jimmy died." The old man was now weeping. "My heart shattered into a million pieces the day I received the news. I don't know what to do with my grief, and I don't want to be hateful, but I'm a parent, a heartbroken father."

A long moment of silence passed as the team held a sacred space for Mr. Sinclair's pain.

Dr. Salam broke the silence by saying softly, "I'll follow your lead, Mr. Sinclair. I'd love to continue to work with you, if you allow it, but I totally understand if you'd rather not. I'll do whatever makes you feel respected, safe, and comfortable."

"Oh, Dr. Salam, please accept my sincere apology," he

replied, looking the young physician right in the eyes. "It isn't you, my daughter. It's everything that's going on. The crazy world we live in. Can you kindly stop by after you're done with your rounds? Let's get to know each other better. And Dr. Johnson, thank you for standing up for your teammates. That's the definition of a true leader."

"It would be my absolute pleasure, Mr. Sinclair," said Dr. Salam, with a big smile, "And thank you very much for opening your heart and sharing Jimmy with us this morning."

Outside the patient's room, Brad said in amazement, "Well, I don't know how you do it, Dr. Salam. I don't think I'd have the same amount of grace if I was in your shoes. People tell me that I make a big fuss out of nothing when I tell them that hate is alive and well in America. Some staff, even on our team, argue with me that the racism issue is blown out of proportion." He shook his head in disbelief. "I guess they've seen it now with their own eyes. I'm also glad you spoke up, Dr. Johnson. I was about to yell at him at the top of my lungs."

"Brad," said Dr. Salam, "you're so very kind, as always. I just happen to believe that violence doesn't solve anything." She shrugged her shoulders. "I'd rather spend my energy educating people about the beauty that comes with diversity. And you've seen that Mr. Sinclair's painful remarks were caused by a deep wound."

"Well, I try to empathize with the old fellow. I also believe that trauma that happens to you can explain, but can never excuse, you traumatizing others," said Brad, annoyed.

"Hate is ugly," said Dr. Johnson. "It forces us into narrow corners where we see each other as enemies. Some of our neighbors and coworkers face this kind of hateful treatment every day."

"I'm sorry you've to put up with this Dr. Salam. I can only imagine how exhausting it must be," said Brad, adding, "I come from a Jewish background. I went through many struggles as a foster kid before I was adopted. My family has been through a lot." He paused reflectively and said with pride, "That's why I'll always speak up on behalf of my coworkers of all backgrounds. Wrong is always wrong even if it's popular, and there's nothing cool about hate. It's way outdated and out of style."

"Thank you, Brad. Our work environment is toxic and stressful enough as it is. The least we can do is not traumatize people because of our own bias and prejudices. Even better, if our words and actions can be a remedy and a source of healing," sighed Dr. Salam. "And if we don't confront aggression, it'll turn into transgression and eventually violence. I've seen it over and over again, and frankly I'm sick and tired of it."

"You're absolutely right," said Brad, shaking his head in agreement. "It's such a blessing to be working with you, Dr. Salam. I love your spirit. And please know that this team is your family."

"Thank you, Brad. You guys are indeed my second family."

Later in the day, Brad smiled as he saw Mr. Sinclair and Dr. Salam showing each other pictures of their loved ones on their phones, and silently weeping as they held hands in prayer.

Driving home, Brad reflected on his own life and wondered what family really meant to him. He felt guilty about his style of relating to his small family. He knew that being abandoned by his biological parents was a very deep wound that he never nursed or tended to. He turned to alcohol instead. "Whenever I drink," he thought, "I numb the pain and shut off the demons, but it's not working. I can do better. The children avoid me because I'm always angry, and I don't know how Rachel still puts up with me. She works long hours too, and then comes home to two kids, one of them with many special needs that require the attention of both his mom and dad. I can, and I will, do better. If someone coming from a war zone can be so graceful, then I'll work harder on finding grace for my story and also for that of my family. They deserve better." Now tearful, yet determined, Brad went to the store to buy roses, hot chocolate, and popcorn. "No alcohol tonight. I'll spend my time and energy where I'm supposed to."

Trauma can manifest in different ways. Hurt people hurt people. Mr. Sinclair's words of hate were coming from a place of deep pain, and Brad's behavior toward his family was the result of an unacknowledged open wound. Leaning in and reaching out are powerful tools that can make a huge difference in the way we relate to our clients and our loved ones.

Boundaries Protect

Taking care of our boundaries can help the helper to not only be better able to help but also find joy in the relationship. Holding space for others can protect them from despair and from giving up, but make sure that your own boundaries are protected. To extend ourselves in every direction leaves nothing for us to give. Every bit of beauty I find in my encounters with clients touches both our hearts, because when our souls are at peace, we are better able to search for and discover, beauty in other souls.

To hold space for others can bring them back to life. Make sure there is room for you, too, in that space.

The caregiver–patient relationship is sacred and needs protecting.

Caregiver fatigue and trauma can intrude on that special bond and interfere with its dynamics. We build and protect sacred connections with people when we are aware of their needs, and of our own.

There is power in sharing. Many therapeutic effects can result from storytelling. We need to watch our reactions to those opening their hearts to us so we can hold and treasure their secrets. Countertransference not only is a psychoanalytic concept about how clients make us feel, but also describes the deep emotions triggered in us when we bear witness to pain. I excuse myself from heavily emotional encounters at times so I can shed tears and regain my composure before returning, better able to listen and bear witness.

We need to learn what we can and cannot influence. Our role as caregivers is to bear witness and resist the wish to "fix" people. We honor the stories of others, but we do not own them.

Be aware of your desire to help everyone you meet, but focus your energy on those you can realistically and meaningfully help. Utilize someone you trust to function as an anchor for your emotional fatigue and moral distress.

I remember a client telling me, after we had worked through an episode of delirium, "What you did for me is nothing less than divine," but there was nothing magical about our relationship. All I did was offer him an emotionally available presence and nonjudgmental listening. It is amazing how easy it is to comfort people and mend their wounded hearts. He touched the hand of the divine and was able to see the face of God in our encounter.

One of the joys that come with caregiving is experiencing gratitude. It makes all the difference when a client says, "I could've never recovered this well if it wasn't for you," or "I truly believe that you guys have saved my life." Very recently, as she was leaving the hospital, one of my patients said, "This was the best place I've ever been, I think my parents should come here too." She was not sarcastic; rather, serious.

Sometimes, staff use humor to navigate difficult encounters. A nurse on the medical floor paged me and requested I consult on one of her patients. I could hear her giggle while saying, "We can use your help with this patient, Dr. Reda. There are UFOs flying in his room." It turned out that he was throwing urine and feces at the nurses and was refusing to cooperate with medical care. I pleaded with the nurse. "Why me? What have I done to you? How about you request someone else see this patient?" But she insisted, citing my "soft voice, calm demeanor, and experience with trauma." So I wore a gown, goggles, and other protective gear and went to see him. I read in his chart that he was a retired veteran who lost his leg in an explosion while on active duty. I greeted him, introduced myself, and asked him why the staff was intimidated by someone who seemed like a gentleman. He said that no one should be afraid of him, especially not female staff, and that he was proud of his career as someone who protected and served the country. We agreed on conditions of a care plan that allowed him to feel more heard and respected without resorting to violence, and the unidentified objects finally stopped flying around his room.

When working with trauma survivors, it is important to see the problem behavior as only the message. I do not judge my patients based on their symptoms but instead I see the behavior as only the message, a cry for help; its origin is likely much deeper. I look at the whole picture, the context, the unmet need, the untold story, the silenced voice, the human behind the labels, and the child longing to be found, held, and comforted.

Here is a story to illustrate some of that.

"Mr. Ramadan, touch me, kiss me, hold me, let's get married." One of my patients kept referring to me as "Mr. Ramadan." Her manic episode had lasted for several weeks. She was extremely exhausted and exhausting. She was delirious to the point that I had to send her to the intensive care unit so she might get some induced sleep, which she desperately needed. The staff assigned to her hourly care had to rotate every 15 minutes, given her excessive amount of energy. She was a sleepless nightmare. She would make nonstop sexual remarks and seductive advances toward all staff, men and women alike. Through all of that, her mother kept saying, "That isn't who she is." This mother wanted us to get to know her daughter as a human, not just as a psychotic or manic patient; but rather, as someone who deserves to be treated with dignity and respect. When it came to compassionate care, my team went above and beyond. They would even lotion and massage her feet and tuck her in to bed, as that was the only way she would doze off for a few minutes. After the mania was finally over, fatigued staff hugged and cried with her and her parents on their way out of the hospital. The hospital staff had helped transform her life, and she in turn had deeply touched theirs.

When working with traumatized clients, we can help their trauma in the same ways we can help our own. Here are some suggestions from the Center for Adolescent Studies:

Describe the trauma through their eyes, and look at the bigger picture and the context, rather than punishing the behavior.

The key point is to step outside of our ego and not take their issues personally. The behavior could be a defense or a protective mechanism on their part. We should avoid reacting to reactions. This leads to less burnout and makes us more available to be present as our most authentic self.

Authentic relationships build and foster interpersonal safety. We should always try to show up as our most consistent, predictable, and genuine self. We, not the intervention, are the healing tools.

Caregivers can look with compassion, or even with awe, at a client's challenging behavior. This is not an easy task at all. It takes discipline and lots of patience and practice for us to pause and think of an appropriate, safe, and healthy response, rather than to quickly and impulsively react to a reaction.

I remember walking into the inpatient unit where I work to find staff ready to inject an agitated Black man with a tranquilizer or place him into seclusion. I asked if I could talk to him first. As I listened to the pain expressed in his projected anger, he disclosed that he could only work with staff of color because he did not trust "white people." He asked for a menu that respected his cultural needs as a Muslim man who only consumes halal or kosher meat, and he asked if he could be allowed a visit with an Imam so he could learn how to pray again, as it "[had] been a long time since [he] last spoke with God." We ended up not needing restraints or antipsychotics after all. All he needed that morning was human connection. I happened to share aspects of his cultural background and religious beliefs, and that made him feel safe enough to open up to me and eventually start to build some trust with the rest of the team.

It is not always going to be possible to meet all of our clients' cultural and religious needs, but on that particular day that plan worked best.

There are four things to remember when bearing witness to individuals in distress:

1. Authenticity: Our clients will quickly discover if we genuinely care about them.
2. Curiosity: We must show interest in them as humans, not only as statistics, or judge them based on labels assigned to symptoms.

3. Flexibility: We must be ready to adjust our way of thinking, and in doing so, be better able to meet their unique needs.
4. Humility: We must maintain an attitude of a student, keen to learn from each encounter.

I remember a young woman who was admitted to the hospital and given the label of schizophrenic because she was hearing voices, but I could feel there was something more to her story, so I inquired about the nature of her auditory hallucinations, and she told me that she was hearing women screaming in her sleep. I decided to dig deeper into her past, and she told me that her father had died in a car accident when she was 10 years old and this was all she knew about the way he passed. But when she had recently turned 18, her mother told her, "By the way, your dad was drunk when he crashed into another car, and two young women died that day." She was hearing their screams terrorizing her sleep. I asked what she had done since learning about the details of the car accident, and she said, "I've been on a mission to find the families of those young ladies, so I can apologize to them on my father's behalf."

What a heavy burden she had placed on her shoulders at that tender young age. No wonder she went psychotic. That is not schizophrenia, though. These are the shadows of trauma. When we hide skeletons in our closets, they tend to come out at times of distress in the form of flashbacks and nightmares. That is why it is important to deeply listen, because if we miss or dismiss the trauma story, we might miss the accurate "diagnosis" and come up with a totally wrong care plan.

Combating Stress

Combat is a term used commonly in the context of war and armed conflict. Some of my colleagues suggested I call this book *The Warrior Healer* rather than *The Wounded Healer*. We are indeed warrior healers. I decided to stick with the current title, however, because a wound for me is a mark of courage, not a sign of weakness. To be wounded is a privilege, not a judgment.

A tool I created to combat stress when working with trauma survivors is the SGP principles (making Space, offering Grace, and respecting Pace). I find this tool to be a helpful approach in many contexts and with people from diverse backgrounds.

Making space means that the healing environment needs to be one that is inviting (beauty focused), inclusive (justice focused), and interpersonally safe (connection focused). Both I, as a caregiver, and the individuals, families, and communities I care for, need to feel safe around each other. Safety is not a given, especially when there is trauma in the background. Rather, it is a culture we build together when we focus on trust, validation, and empowerment. Trust builds safety, and vice versa. We should not assume that people will trust us with their deep feelings just because of our profession; we need to earn that trust. It is an honor to be trusted.

Here is an example of how earning our clients' trust needs to always be on our minds, and how traumatic memories can be triggered in the safety of the therapeutic space.

One day during my residency training in psychiatry, one of my long-term psychodynamic psychotherapy patients was visibly restless. I felt that there was something in the room that was making her agitated, that her discomfort was in our interpersonal space and in the dynamics of our relationship. She tried to dismiss my curiosity, but when I insisted, she shared that my new cologne was making her uncomfortable because it was the same brand that her grandfather was wearing when he sexually assaulted her. What activates traumatic memories can be very subtle indeed. That is why we need to be emotionally attuned to those we care for. One powerful tool to achieving that goal is self-attunement.

Offering grace is showing care and compassion toward self and others. This comes from unconditionally respecting the basic dignity and shared humanity of everyone, and being both decent and graceful when confronted with different beliefs, practices, and viewpoints. Caregivers interact with people from all walks of life. Patients come from diverse backgrounds and belief systems, and they may engage in behaviors that caregivers disagree with. What matters is for us to have the attitude of a student and ask our clients to teach and educate us.

Respecting pace can be tricky to navigate. On the one hand, it is true that we cannot force or expedite healing and that we need to respect people's style and speed of their recovery journeys. Yet on the other hand, it is important not to remain silent when witnessing someone struggling alone. To make sure that we are neither intrusive nor neglectful of human suffering is an art that is worth mastering. I see that commonly in a family context. When trauma impacts the household, family members might see each other as enemies, and that risks breaking the family unit. We will expand on this further in the next chapter, which covers the impact of trauma on our families.

Even though some healers use dissociation as a defense mechanism to protect themselves from deep and strong emotions, they continue to aid clients in discovering root causes of their issues and in helping them find hidden strength and beauty. Behind the mask of caregiving is a healer who helps people

- find safety: through fostering hope in the future and instilling faith in humanity;
- find voice: by building safe spaces and giving people "permission" to talk;
- find meaning: by working with survivors of trauma on repairing shattered core beliefs about safety, trust, and common goodness, and helping them realize that they are not broken because of the trauma they endured;
- find forgiveness: through emphasizing unconditional self-forgiveness, which might mean making and receiving amends, and helping those we care for appreciate that they have done their best given the circumstances. We need to respect the pace of recovery journeys, especially when it comes to exploring forgiveness of predators and perpetrators of horrific traumatic acts like incest, torture, and genocide. People should not feel pressured to forgive others, what is important is forgiving oneself;
- find healing: by harnessing resilience, promoting self-care, and encouraging altruism and community service;
- find closure: through helping them mourn past relationships and redefine or reconstruct new ones; and
- find beauty: by way of integrating the trauma story so they may find beauty in themselves, in their families, in others, and in the world all around them. There is beauty despite suffering.

Behind the mask also is a human, not a superhero, and not a machine, but a human who has emotions and has basic needs that deserve to be fulfilled. One way to do that is to "not take your clients home with you." Separating work life from personal life is a sign of good self-care.

We signed up to be healers, not victims.

Working With Resistance

The concept of self-awareness helps when working with resistant "problem" clients. This is something I was grateful to learn from Dr. Sam Himelstein and his colleagues at the Center for Adolescent Studies. Ongoing preventive self-care for caregivers involves achieving distance from the negativity of a situation by viewing a "difficult" person as lacking the needed social and coping skills and sending them compassion.

When working with resistance, what we see is the tip of an iceberg (the visible problematic behaviors) and not what is beneath the surface (the root causes of the pain and distress). It is important to see the bigger picture (the context), to examine your internal state (through self-awareness and self-management), and then to use a skillful intervention (engagement). For example, if a patient physically or sexually "acts out," we need to look at the context. Maybe that is their adaptation to witnessing domestic violence or to enduring sexual trauma as children. That approach will take our ego out of the situation, so we can then refocus and be better able to engage more skillfully with the client, leading to a more favorable outcome for all involved.

Resistance is the protective armor that gets activated when we feel threatened. Seeing trauma through that lens will remove the caregiver's emotional investment from the equation, which will improve the response. The more you take yourself out of your clients' emotional turmoil, the more you respond rather than react to their reactions, and the more you align with them and get them connected with their deep internal state.

Himelstein warns:

> If you see it the other way, that resistance is only negative and represents the true character of the client, then you will react

rather than respond, you will take things personally and engage unskillfully, leading to more resistance. It is therefore key when resistance arises that we resist our own urge to take it personally or react in ways that assert our authority. When a staff engages in a power struggle with their patient, it is a lose-lose situation. The patient misses out on having their basic need (the source of the behavior) met, and the staff member feels bad about using a punitive approach that does not align with the way they enjoy caregiving. (Himelstein & Gonzalez, n.d.)

Sometimes our own shadows can cast darkness on the therapeutic encounter. In one case I know of, a patient threatened a staff, triggering the staff member's PTSD from his time in Iraq. The staff ended up slamming the patient to the floor. If we do not nurse our deep wounds, they might bleed in ways that surprise or hurt us and those around us.

Apply mindfulness instead. Less ego means more skillfulness. When you take your ego out, you suffer less and have less compassion fatigue and vicarious trauma.

When encountering a case of resistant, "difficult" behavior, you can use one or more of these tools:

- TAP: Take a deep breath and pause to examine your thoughts, acknowledge your feelings, and proceed with a behavior that aligns with your values.
- STOP: Literally stop; take a deep breath; observe the context, your emotional status and your options; then proceed skillfully.
- RAIN: Recognize, acknowledge, investigate, and nurture your experience.

- STIC: Stop, take a deep breath, imagine future consequences, and choose your next action consciously.
- SIFT: Examine your sensations, images, feelings, and thoughts. Envision a conceptual map of your subjective experience, then act in a way that is authentic for you.

The Therapeutic Power of Listening

Listening is a powerful pathway to healing. Not everybody is ready to tell their story. We should not force or pressure people to tell their stories when they are not ready. But if they are ready, then we should open our ears, eyes, hearts, and souls to listen, understand, and deeply appreciate—again, to offer space, not to fix. If we do not feel that we can hear them, then we need to have resources available, and refer them to someone who might be better able, or more ready, to listen.

Also remember that most people do not have to tell the minute, graphic details of what happened to them in order to heal. What matters is that the elephant in the room gets acknowledged and that people be given a voice, a platform, and permission to coherently reclaim their narrative.

When working with a Syrian refugee boy, I saw that he showed significant improvement in all his anxiety symptoms through the use of art and play therapy, with one exception: he did not stop fidgeting. My colleagues and I found out during a home visit that every day he massaged his father's hands. His dad had been shot by a sniper during the Syrian armed conflict, and the bullet shattered his spinal cord, rendering him quadriplegic. The fidgeting was the boy's desperate attempt to take away his father's suffering and erase the horrific memories. He said, "Maybe one day I can hug my dad." That amount of resilience and coping was elicited without the need for me to dig deep into the traumatic material or ask about the graphic details of the actual incident, which could have risked retraumatizing the beautiful boy.

We should focus on the human spirit and the resilience of trauma survivors, and share in the celebration of their culture, coping skills, and potential for healing and beauty.

A patient I worked with through an episode of psychosis concluded our session with a heartwarming message that made coming to work every day absolutely worth it. He announced that my "mere presence" made him feel safer. It seems that when I reached out to the human in him, buried under the multiple layers of medical jargon and the heavy labels of symptoms and psychiatric diagnoses, and when I treated him with the dignity and respect that he deserved, in return he was able to touch my heart with his genuine humanity and beautiful words of appreciation and gratitude.

Being authentic means being true to those we serve, and also being true to ourselves. According to the Center for Adolescent Studies, here are a few ways we can give our best to others without getting depleted:

- Caregivers should always strive to establish authentic relationships. Authentic communication interventions include starting with a question, not a command (ask what purpose the resistance serves), using a skillful tone, bringing awareness about the resistance being a protective mechanism, and expressing our feelings in the here and now when appropriate.
- Giving requires boundaries. Yes, it is okay to want to give more than you get, but live well and take care of yourself and your family. That will mean setting firm boundaries at times and, yes, knowing when to say no.
- Caregivers need to attune to their needs through self-awareness and to recognize the stress they feel and find ways to address it.

If you are feeling like you are floating in an ocean of distress, look for anchors. Start with simple self-care activities and small acts of kindness. Set smart and realistic goals—for example, a healthy meal, one more cup of water, extra time for sleep or exercise, a quality time with a friend or loved ones—and then build on that.

I hope that by now you have seen and appreciated how intricate and complicated are the sacred relationships caregivers have with their clients. This special bond makes us continue to look with awe at the power of love and the potential for healing and transformation that comes with compassionate and authentic interventions, even with people who are deeply trauma- *Take care of yourself, because if you don't no one else will.* tized. Furthermore, I hope you have realized that the field of caring can bring a burden to our hearts and make our souls ache. Yet, if we can strike a healthy balance between the needs of those we serve and our own needs, and if we see self-care as a responsibility rather than a luxury, and if we take the time to nurse our wounds and honor our trauma story, we will be better able to not only care for people but also find joy doing it.

Habits That Can Help Healers Heal

Caregivers usually take care of others before themselves. We are experts in putting the needs of everyone else before our needs. We go the extra mile to spend every ounce of energy on our patients, leaving us only enough gas in our emotional tanks to crash into our beds. And yes, tomorrow is another day to repeat the deadly cycle. Even cars do not run on empty tanks. It is important that we find ways to rejuvenate and leave some gas in our tank for tomorrow's journey.

An interesting phenomenon noticeable in our field is that caregivers find it difficult to accept thanks. They quickly dismiss praise with phrases like "It was just my job," "That's what I'm supposed to do," "It's not that big a deal." But it is really not a sign of healthy humility to reject praise or give the credit for your hard work to others.

The first law of medicine is to "do no harm." That means to do no harm to ourselves as well.

You cannot solve a problem if you pretend it never existed.

So why do caregivers put their own needs last? Caregivers I talked with came up with fascinating excuses to justify ranking their needs at the bottom of their to-do list and placing themselves at the back of the line. These "reasons" include:

- "There's always someone who needs me more than I need the break."
- "When I'm impatient or not as giving and forgiving as I should be for patients who really just need my grace, I doubt that I'm a good-enough person."
- "I feel guilty taking time for myself. I work so much, and I have so many things to take care of at home. I feel like taking time away from my family is selfish. I'm not at a place yet where I feel ready to do it." It is always "not the right time" with caregivers who feel guilty for taking time to tend to even the most basic of their needs. But there is no such concept as the right time; seize the current moment and make it right.
- "I don't reach out to colleagues for fear of traumatizing them."
- "Everyone around me feels the weight of it. If I'm unloading my stuff onto them, they've to carry my weight, and that's not fair. But I'll be there expecting others to unload their emotional garbage on me, and I feel comfortable carrying their weight."

There exists a breaking point, and we all have one. (Wible, 2016)

Ironically, struggling alone and enduring silent suffering are rampant in the field of caring. Some caregivers I interviewed attributed their not speaking up to deeply held beliefs and unsupportive cultures that negatively impact morale. Examples of these personal and systemic dysfunctions include:

- "I experience the gossip and hear the judgment when someone shows tenderness."
- "It's a fine balance caring for my patients' issues without owning them."
- "Sometimes it's difficult to remove my caregiver's hat when I see suffering."
- "We're expected to solve our own problems, and feeling bad makes me question my competence."
- "We're in the middle of a permanent trauma zone. The stress is never-ending."
- "I fear most what's between my ears. Caregivers are the best ruminators."
- "It's in the silence that the monster breeds."
- "Everyone deserves someone. I know that in my head, but it doesn't seem to register in my heart. I don't want to show vulnerability."
- "Many people don't empathize with our suffering. We're viewed as privileged."

Suppressed feelings lead to a lack of self-awareness. Expressing an emotion can re-channel some of the energy it evokes in us and processing a memory can take away some of its power to scare us; hence the importance of acknowledging and skillfully listening to the trauma story.

I recently took care of a patient who was described as "racist." I treated him with dignity and compassion. He was quite wounded, having experienced childhood sexual trauma and the suicide of his best friend. He said that lashing out was his way of not getting hurt again. We were able to work through, and overcome, some of our perceived differences. That encounter reminded me of the story of a veteran who was angry at Black people because his best friend, who was Black, had killed himself shortly after they spent the day together. Making him find compassion for his friend and for himself took reframing by another member of the group therapy session who pointed out, "Your friend found no one better to spend his last few moments with. That is a friend whose life is to be celebrated, not one we stay angry with."

Everyone is fighting a hard fight.

Smink (2018) reminds us that caregivers can be too busy with the outside noise to listen to what is stirring within. They decline the invitation to lean in and look within because "it is too painful to go there." Dysfunctional and maladaptive patterns then develop over time, and stories get buried under layers of taboo that hinder the capacity for healing. Many caregivers have no idea how to get in touch with their feelings. They either dismiss strong emotions or numb them. It will serve all of us well if caregivers master the emotional intelligence, vocabulary, and literacy that will enable them to process their big feelings, and if they learn the skills they need to nurse their bleeding wounds.

Bottled-up emotions, when expressed, may surprise us. We try to hold it together, but then we explode or shut down, and turn into the type of monster we hate. That is how we learn that it is dangerous to feel, but that is also exactly why we should learn to feel and become comfortable expressing our feelings. We should not be the reason that our patients, our loved ones, and our coworkers are terrified or why they walk on eggshells around us. The world is a cruel and often scary place. The least we can do is to make our interpersonal encounters places of safety, always, for everyone we come in contact with.

Self-Care

Self-care is vital to preventing provider burnout and compassion fatigue. You cannot meaningfully care for others if you do not take care of yourself as well. Healers need to know their limits and be assertive and mindful about not carrying a load heavier than what they can realistically handle. Self-care is not selfish. It is tending to the needs of others while observing what is happening within. Listen, evaluate, and problem-solve, not only to benefit others but also to enhance your own soul's health.

I now feel comfortable asserting my needs and boundaries with the people I serve, and no longer feel guilty doing it. Even with my community work after hours and on weekends, I tell people that I will be turning my cell phone off at 9 p.m. For emergencies after hours, they need to dial 911, call the crisis line, or go to the nearest emergency room. I cannot be on call 24 hours a day, 7 days a week, 365 days a year—that would be insanity, professional suicide. No human can do that, nor should anyone feel obligated to.

Self-care is especially key during times of stress. According to the World Health Organization (2020):

- Grounding yourself in the face of an emotional storm does not make the storm disappear but makes you safe until it passes. You can move toward your values when you do these:
  - Pay attention, be attuned, enjoy the world around you, engage with and focus on the current moment, observe difficult feelings with curiosity and compassion, and welcome your shadows as brief guests.

- Slow down and reconnect with your body, mind, heart, and soul, and engage the five senses. One effective grounding exercise when feeling stressed-out is to bring yourself to the current moment and live in the here and now by engaging your faculties. (Focus on your immediate surroundings: what are five things you see, four things you hear, three things you feel, two things you smell, and one thing you taste?)

- Unhooking: Notice and name difficult thoughts and feelings that "hook" you. This brings awareness to them. Then refocus on the current moment and choose to act on your values of caring for yourself, your family, and your community. We are all hooked by tears about yesterday or fears about tomorrow. In order to get unhooked, we need to enjoy today and treat it as a gift. Do not wait for the "perfect moment"; live the current one. Live your life in every detail. Live life despite the pain. The world can bring suffering, but it can also be a source of great joy.

- Engaging: Most human suffering happens within relationships. It is important, therefore, that we heal our relational wounds through healing our interpersonal relations.

- Acting on your values: You can always love your values, even when traumatized. Acting on them is a choice whatever the circumstances. Ask the question, "Do my actions support my values?" Caring and kindness toward others and self puts your values into action. As caregivers, we get traumatized by our industry every day. We can act in hostility and retaliate, or we can appeal to our best version of ourselves and engage authentically.

- Being kind, especially to yourself: When unkind thoughts hook you, they pull you away from your values. Caregivers are masters when it comes to self-loathing. When we make a small mistake, we view that as the end of the world and see ourselves as a failure. It is important that we break that cycle.

- Making room: No matter how severe the weather, the sky has room for it without the sky getting hurt. Sooner or later the weather will improve, and the rainbow will come out with all its majestic colors and mesmerizing beauty. Breathing around your pain makes room for it. Difficult feelings are like words in a book: You can tuck the book under your arm and take it with you but still engage with the world around you. Stop fighting your pain. Notice it and give it space. Imagine your hand full of kindness and place it on the source of pain. Even in the face of tremendous adversity, you can find meaning, purpose, and vitality in your life. Children and adults can navigate through difficult trauma dynamics when they befriend their shadows and when they get comfortable naming and taming big feelings.

Making self-care a priority and taking care of yourself is always the right thing to do if you are to continue to function as a caregiver. We can and we will fall apart if we do not take care of ourselves. Our first reaction to this advice is often "When will I ever find the time to relax?"— *We see ourselves as failures when we lose one patient, even if we save thousands. (Wible, 2016)* but it is amazing how little time it takes to refresh ourselves. Our body and spirit thrive on small acts of kindness. What can you do right now to insert a gentle dose of self-care into your day? Do exactly that.

The 5 Rs (a helpful tool to remind you of your own needs)

- Recognize the need for a break.
- Request or demand a break.
- Relax during your break (unfortunately, it is common for many caregivers to be spending their breaks engaging in stressful activities).
- Realize your priorities (when there is too much on your plate, learn to prioritize, minimize, and downsize). Learn to set realistic goals, then celebrate small victories.
- Reengage more refreshed, reenergized, and recentered.

According to the Center for Adolescent Studies:

Self-care leads to internal predictability even if the external world is unpredictable. It includes not only regular relaxation activities, but also fruitful training, creative expression, and social bonding. Self-care should be proactive, not reactive. Self-care done routinely develops predictability and proficiency. To consistently use self-care tools eventually builds resilience, through leaning-in (mindfulness, prayer, and positive affirmations) and leaning-out (exercise and hobbies). The more your intrapersonal attunement, the better you become at interpersonal attunement.

Mindful meditation

It is said that meditation is cheaper than medication and has fewer side effects, and that if you keep reciting the mantra in your head, eventually you will feel it in your heart. Meditation is not merely the act of sitting in silence but, rather, mindful reflection and deep introspection.

According to Professor Richard Mollica (2018) of the Harvard Program in Refugee Trauma:

> Grounding is like an anchor; water is calmer on the bottom even if the surface water is rough. For meditation, it is not only the external noises that need to be quieted, but mainly the internal thoughts and judgments. When you meditate and mindfully reflect, you start to reconnect with the aspects of yourself you feel you are losing. Mindful meditation is practiced in solitude but has the potential to be one of the most important connection tools. Meditation can be a powerful relational practice.

Mindfulness is about being with, not necessarily about calming, the experience. One fruit of mindfulness is a skillful frame of mind, the realization that the other person is hurting and trying to protect themselves, that this is not about me. I will practice mindful self-management in the moment, then engage skillfully to align with the client, bringing them self-awareness and deepening the relationship.

Mollica (2018) helped coin the term *empathic meditation* to remind us that "Meditation and empathy together can co-construct the healing experience." Self-empathy, he urges, leads to lower distress and subsequently more empathy toward clients.

Recovery is to recover the aspects of you that are lost to trauma. Recovery requires healthy skills, including the 5-Cs

- commitment (intentionality),
- connection (support),

- coping with difficult emotions,
- care (self-care), and
- claiming one's own narrative (making sense of suffering)

Acknowledge your own trauma, and know your ACEs score

Caregivers need to be aware of their own dark shadows and buried skeletons. It is easier to be labeled as anxious or depressed and get started on medications than to sit in discomfort wrestling with difficult emotions, looking the past right in the eye and telling it that it has no power to ruin your future or spoil the current moment.

Unresolved trauma in the caregiver might get provoked by patients' trauma stories. This is especially true when trauma happens to children. Childhood trauma strikes a chord in us, perhaps because we firmly hold on to core beliefs that the world should be a place of safety for children and that adults are to be trusted to care for them. Interpersonal violence and man-made trauma, especially of an "intimate" nature like sexual violation, affect us much more deeply than the large-scale destruction of natural disasters and even the trauma of living through a global pandemic. We need to be aware of, and work through, our old and unfinished business.

A word about the adverse childhood experiences (ACEs) score: As a caregiver, you would be well advised to know your ACEs score, and I urge you to, not just to ruminate about a number but to honor the experience. In the words of Bruce Perry (2021), "The number is not your story." One of the initial tools for assessing trauma is to score on a scale of 0 to 10 the number of traumatic events you encountered before the age of 18. The list is by no means exhaustive. You can see that severe interpersonal traumatic events like terrorism, torture, kidnapping, community violence, forced displacement, and racism are not part of the traditional ACEs. The 10 traumatic experiences included in the original ACEs study are

- emotional abuse,
- physical abuse,
- sexual abuse,
- emotional neglect,
- physical neglect,
- parental separation or divorce,
- domestic violence,
- parental substance abuse,
- household mental illness, and
- parental incarceration.

A high score is not a reason to judge yourself or to panic. It is just a reminder for you that unprocessed trauma can get activated at times of distress.

Trauma does not happen only to children; it can happen to people at any age. Most of my trauma happened during my adult years. In 2011, my home country, Libya, went through a brutal, bloody war. I still remember vividly the morning of March 19, 2011, when the army received orders for the whole city of Benghazi to be wiped out. I was about to witness a genocide, the extermination of my hometown, and the annihilation of 750,000 people, including my whole family. I remember talking to my mom over the phone and her telling me that she loved me, that she was proud of me, and that we would meet again in heaven. No child should ever have to hear those words from their mother. The trepidation in her voice haunted me for many restless nights and terrorized my sleep.

I had many losses in that nonsensical, protracted conflict. Two of my cousins were killed by the government's armed forces, and my nephew was executed by a terrorist group, leaving behind a beautiful daughter who was yet to turn one. War is ugly. The loudest noise you hear during wars is the sound of broken hearts.

I decided to be aware of how much trauma I had endured and to use my pain to engage in healing others, keeping in mind that I needed to also care for myself because I would certainly meet some of my old shadows along the way.

The higher the ACEs score, the more severe the possible negative impacts on physical and mental health and on psychosocial wellness. Findings from the ACEs study showed higher levels of heart disease, cancer, depression, and suicide, and a reduction in life expectancy. There are many factors, nature and nurture, that can mitigate this. Caregivers who are adult survivors of childhood trauma need to acknowledge and address their pain to be able to effectively nurse the wounds of others without theirs getting reopened. My colleagues' traumas get activated when a patient shares a story similar to theirs. After losing my mother to dementia in 2016, I began seeing her beloved face in the faces of all my elderly patients.

Unlike acute stress, chronic stress can have health-damaging, rather than lifesaving, consequences. There are many hormones and chemicals involved in responding to adversity, especially that of protracted nature. The hormone adrenaline (also known as epinephrine) is commonly known as the emergency hormone. It helps us anticipate, and prepare for, threats through activating the fight-or-flight response. That is helpful, and even critical in the short term, but it can have long-lasting negative health consequences if we remain for a long time in a state of arousal, fearing an actual or perceived threat. The hormone cortisol is commonly called the stress hormone. It helps us respond to acute stress, but it can be harmful in the long run, impacting our blood pressure, blood sugar, gut, and immune system.

An unacknowledged trauma story leaves its imprints on our DNA and on the way it is read and transcribed, which risks perpetuating the impacts of trauma transgenerationally. That is why it is important to try to prevent, screen for, and heal trauma. We do it for ourselves, but we also owe it to our loved ones.

As a caregiver, I urge you to
- look with compassion at, and nurse, your wounds;
- learn to slow down;
- examine your priorities;
- not lose sight of what is important;
- practice gratitude;
- engage in acts of service;
- join a community of care, or build your own; and
- use all available resources.

Sharing our stories, sharing our pain

According to Edward Smink (2018), "The soul's voice needs to be heard through reflection and storytelling. Reconnecting to the soul leads to discovery of inner issues but also hidden resources. Pain scars, but also refines, the soul."

Smink (2018) urges, "If we do not share our pain, we might be sitting with the discomfort of empty feelings, numb to what is going on inside. Interior walls built for protection debilitate us. Walls are only healthy if they serve as self-care boundaries." Let us start building bridges that connect and demolish walls that separate.

After my mother died in 2016, I literally lost my voice for several weeks. Mom was my best friend, and I needed to internally process that deep heartache before I could externally share it with my wife, who was there to gracefully listen, hold, witness, absorb, and share that heavy burden with me. To be able to process your trauma with someone you trust is a divine gift.

Things I found helpful to managing my own PTSD resulting from compassion:

- leaning on my faith (both religion and spirituality)
- paying attention to, and holding dear, my family and loved ones (relationships)
- engaging in community causes, teaching, and education (service)
- enjoying the outdoors and writing (personal healing activities)
- practicing gratitude (soul remedy)

Sharing can turn memories from painful to empowering or even transformative. The caregiving experience can feed, or eat at, our soul. Speaking up has a way of chasing the monsters of silence away.

One day, my youngest daughter, who is usually a very happy and bubbly child, was giving us lots of attitude and was in a very foul mood. I decided to practice what I preach. I reminded her that we live in a safe house, that we have an open-door policy, and that we share big feelings and do not wrestle with them alone. She was able through that approach to regain her voice and tell me what was on her mind. A few minutes of "time-in" might sound like the long way to resolving an issue, but it has proved to be a shortcut. For the sake of my children, I will humble myself and learn new tools. For their sake, I will even walk through blazing fires.

I see that approach work well with my children, and I also see it work wonders with my clients. We all deserve to have our voices heard and our stories honored. Listening with understanding and deep appreciation is a healing gift that we should offer one another.

Dr. Mollica (2018) says that "Storytelling is considered a verbal meditation." *Meditation* and *medicine* share the root *med*, which is Greek for "care." One benefit of meditation is patience (which means the process of going through suffering). Empathic meditation is taking an intentional, empathic, and attentional look at the self. As we use LUDA (Listening with Understanding and Deep Appreciation) with our clients, let us apply it to ourselves. Storytelling can be an extremely powerful healing tool.

But listening to the stories of others can be draining. A ship sinks not because of the big body of water around it, but because of the small amount of water that gets inside of it. Similarly, you can be surrounded with lots of negativity, but what affects you is only what you internalize. The depth and time of your exposure to the stories is also important, not only the nature of your profession (for example, a teacher, chaplain, or community leader might get affected more deeply than an actual therapist by the act of listening to traumatic and traumatizing stories).

Resilience

Different people respond differently to stress. That is why it is important to offer ourselves the gift of grit through harnessing resilience. Imagine stress as a pot of boiling water. Some of us are like noodles—we soften and melt into our environment. (There should be no judgment assigned to that style of coping.) Others of us are like eggs—we harden and shield ourselves from our environment. (There should be no judgment placed on that way of coping either.) And a few of us are like coffee beans—we offer our beautiful colors and delicious flavors to actively engage with or change our environment. (And again, with no judgment attached to that coping mechanism.) Many factors contribute to why we behave a certain way when we get traumatized. Factors like having a trusted caring adult or a supportive community can help us harness resilience and build self-esteem.

Trauma can be the driving force to achieving resilience. The Japanese term *Kintsukuroi* means to use gold to repair what is broken, nicely stating that things can become more beautiful when tested with adversity and that people can become stronger and more resilient because of the trauma they endure. Trauma can make, rather than break, us as individuals, families, and communities.

Self-care helps build resilience. Resilience is not only about being able to bounce back but also about being stronger because of what happened. We thrive, not only survive, because of our trauma story. Resilience is the positive adaptation in the face of suffering, leading eventually to meeting one's full potential and discovering hidden beauty. I am always in awe when visiting refugee camps and seeing how children cope with the trauma of war and armed conflict. Their resolve always warms my heart and lifts my spirits.

Factors that can help harness resilience include

- internal assets—like core values, self-worth, and skills (life skills like time management, social skills like teamwork, coping skills like expressing emotions, and survival skills like navigating through a global pandemic); and
- external assets—like social support and empowerment.

Help harness resilience through teaching assertiveness, conflict resolution, problem-solving, and stress management. And remember the human connection. Foundationally, resilience rests on relationships.

Resilience, according to the Center for Adolescent Studies, is the ability to overcome difficulties. Build it through having flexible routines that give a sense of autonomy, and through practicing self-care, not only feeling relaxed but also feeling productive. Also important is social connection. Model practicing self-care for your loved ones and everyone around you. Encourage being flexible, staying connected, and using all lifelines.

Children are quite resilient, and they deserve to have us continue to build on their strengths. Since the 2011 war, I have been back to Libya on seven different occasions. I have also been on humanitarian missions to the Syrian border with Turkey and to the Burmese border with Bangladesh, where the Rohingya refugees are displaced. It is true that there is significant pain and trauma in refugee camps, but there is also lots of resiliency, hope, beauty, and light coming out of those forgotten tents.

Many stories come to mind here, all of them worth sharing. For example, at a "safe space" in Bangladesh for Rohingya refugee parents escaping the genocide in their home country of Burma, the parents shared stories of helplessly watching family members drown or get beaten to death, and feeling broken and humiliated while their villages were set on fire. An Australian volunteer nurse asked me "Dr. Reda, why is it that the Rohingya refugees seem to never have joy?" It is because the trauma story violently takes away from survivors their ability to smile. Children, however, seem to do better when given avenues to express their emotions through play and art therapy activities.

Despite all the trauma these beautiful children have endured, they continue to engage actively in the search for beauty. As caregivers, we can build on that if we look for beauty in every encounter, because there is plenty of it. That is why, despite being an adult psychiatrist, I most enjoy traveling the world, conducting play and art activities with traumatized youth.

People respond to, and heal from, trauma in different ways. It is therefore important to address misconceptions about our role as healers. According to Rev. Samuel Wood (2012), there are false beliefs caregivers hold to that can contribute to compassion fatigue and burnout. For example:

- I will "fix" it . . . make everything right . . . save the world.
- I am responsible for the outcome.
- If I care enough, everything will be okay.
- The sufferer/victim will appreciate everything I do for them.
- I will have enough resources (time, money, materials, skills, training) to fix things.
- Significant people in my life will support and approve of my absence from our relationships while I invest in this compassionate mission.
- I know what I am getting myself into.
- I can do it alone.
- If I am spiritual enough, I can deal with the stress of working with suffering.
- My definition of success is . . .

These beliefs are not only dysfunctional, they can also be dangerous, jeopardizing our health, and in turn negatively impacting the well-being of those we care for.

Caregivers' Compassion Fatigue

Unacknowledged, burnout can lead healers to leave the profession they once loved. I know colleagues who left toxic work environments that used to crush their souls, and ended up following their hearts, joining more-compassionate systems, opening their own healing spaces, or pursuing a passion. They all seem much happier. Refuse to be another statistic. Do not settle for being one more casualty of the cruel system.

Trauma is often missed or dismissed; mislabeled or misdiagnosed as attention deficit hyperactivity disorder (ADHD), oppositional defiant disorder (ODD), borderline personality disorder (BPD), and so on. These labels are like Band-Aids; they cover but they do not cure the deep, bleeding, inflamed, and infected wounds. We do not blindly treat physical conditions; rather, we address the source. Similarly, we should investigate, and not only medicate, the source of trauma.

As helpers, we are terrible at asking for help. Those of us who reach the point of utter hopelessness become unreachable. (Wible, 2016)

There are striking similarities between the symptoms of compassion fatigue and those of post-traumatic stress disorder (PTSD). That is why caregivers' PTSD is referred to as a moral distress rather than a mental disorder.

Stages of compassion fatigue

According to Rev. Samuel Wood (2012), here are the stages of compassion fatigue that we need to pay attention to in order to recognize burnout early and hopefully prevent it.

- The Zealot Phase (the enthusiast): staff is committed and willing to do extra work
- The Irritability Phase (the cynic): staff starts to resent what they do
- The Withdrawal Phase (the loner): staff becomes irritable, pushes loved ones away
- The Zombie Phase: staff is completely burned out, both inside their homes and places of employment

Symptoms of compassion fatigue

According to Rev. Samuel Wood (2012), here are some of the symptoms of compassion fatigue that we need to pay attention to:

- Intrusive symptoms: those include the inability to emotionally and morally distance oneself from their clients' stories
- Avoidance symptoms: for example feeling detached from things that remind us of the pain of our clients
- Arousal symptoms: including being hypervigilant and easily startled

Burnout, a Silent Killer

Burnout is when the pain of listening to the stories of others (vicarious trauma) starts to deeply impact your soul. If you do not tend to that soul ache (compassion fatigue), you might risk exhausting and even depleting your emotional resources, ending in a total burnout. The Maslach Burnout Inventory (MBI) measures:

- emotional exhaustion—the feeling of being emotionally overextended and exhausted caring for others;
- depersonalization—the unfeeling and impersonal response toward patients; and
- personal accomplishment—the feelings of competence and successful achievement in one's work.

Symptoms of compassion fatigue can have a wide variety of characteristics, including somatic, cognitive, emotional, behavioral, academic, vocational, spiritual, interpersonal, or a combination of any or all of those.

Compassion fatigue versus vicarious trauma

If you feel beaten up by listening, that could be a sign of compassion fatigue. If your soul is deeply touched by the stories of others, that might be a sign of vicarious trauma. The two, while very similar, are quite different in that vicarious trauma happens when we listen to stories of pain shared by trauma survivors, while compassion fatigue is the sense of moral exhaustion we feel when we are deeply engaged in the act of emotionally caring for others.

TAKE STEPS TO AVOID CAREGIVER FATIGUE

Tidbits to help you cope with, or reduce, compassion fatigue:

- You are responsible for your part of the task, but not for the outcome.
- The need will always be greater than your resources.
- Use care in how you define and measure "success."
- Value and celebrate the effort, not only the outcome.
- Who you are is more important to the "mission" than what you do.
- Their pain is not yours.
- Stop walking wounded. Start taking breaks to fill your tank. You can't pour from an empty cup.
- Don't own your patients' pain.
- Remember to care for your soul, heart, mind, and body, so there will be something left in you to continue to give.

Secondary traumatization

Secondary trauma is a term used to describe the "activation" of an existing "primary" trauma. In other words, our old wound gets reopened by the new injury. These are some of the factors that can contribute to secondary traumatization:

- caregiver's personality traits like disregarding own boundaries and viewing soul ache as a character flaw or moral failure
- caregiver's mental health history prior to re-traumatization
- nature of the traumatic event
- the meaning assigned to the trauma
- available social and professional support

Posttraumatic recovery and growth can be helped quite a bit by grounding skills; rituals and ceremonies; the use of nature-based, art-based, movement-based, and memory-based interventions; and leaning on family, faith, and social-support networks. When I go to a refugee camp abroad, or work with a local community here in the United States, I try to incorporate the four elements of nature, art, movement, and memories to bring healing to others through hands-on interactive events that aim to empower, rather than enable, participants; and then I try to use four other tools (leaning on my faith, appreciating my family, showing gratitude through searching for and appreciating beauty in others, and engaging in acts of service) to heal myself.

Plan for a healthy lifestyle:
- personal time
- healthy eating habits
- daily exercise routine

- sleep hygiene
- cutting down on the number of responsibilities, especially those not under your control
- limiting the use of technology and sedentary activities
- getting fresh air consistently and enjoying mother nature
- talking about your feelings
- social support (healthy and non-stressful network of friends)
- professional support (colleagues and others like a coach, a therapist, etc.)
- looking after your soul and spiritual needs
- expressing gratitude
- loving your family
- engaging in community service and acts of kindness

Become self-aware. Trauma can shake the psyche and shatter its foundations. It can cast doubt on identity and self-worth and can distort how we view our intrinsic value. I invite caregivers to look behind the mask and past the self-imposed labels so they can get back in touch with, and embrace, their beauty. We need to remind one another daily of how beautiful we are—of all the beauty we bring to our work with clients and our interactions with coworkers, and all the beauty we offer the world. Let us notice people; people blossom when noticed.

Traumatic stress
Trauma means "wound," a significant stress that overwhelms our inner coping resources. Many things make a stressful event traumatic, but it is our perception of an event and the meaning we assign to it that usually affect us the most. For example, the global coronavirus pandemic initially took the sense of safety and control away from us, and its pro-

tracted nature made some people see no end in sight and thereby fall into despair.

Learn physically calming techniques. Severe trauma leads to a chronically activated autonomic nervous system (ANS) and almost complete shutdown of the frontal lobe. Inherently non-clinical relational activities (INCRAs) help regulate internal experiences. Caregivers are usually comfortable using INCRAs with their patients (like joining them on a walk, sharing a meal, playing a card game, engaging in a sport, etc.). We need to use these non-clinical therapeutic tools to calm our own ANS. Whenever a client is clearly upset and getting restless (hyper-aroused), or whenever they are becoming visibly withdrawn and shutting down (hypo-aroused), I invite them to an INCRA. Joining someone at a time of distress can lighten their burden. How about we extend the same invitations and interventions to ourselves?

Coping With Death

Coming to terms with the death of clients or their loved ones is a regular experience for caregivers, and one that they usually dread. Witnessing our clients dying is a highly stressful trauma and disempowering event that we do not talk much about, yet other people, including our loved ones, see us as being perfectly capable of easily handling and coping with the issue of death and dying.

I am in awe when working with teams in areas such as oncology, palliative care, obstetrics, and neonatology, and when I bear witness to my colleagues in the ICU, the ED, and other high-risk units. Losing a new mother or a newborn baby, or feeling powerless watching someone die is a deep moral injury that can linger with these caring souls for quite a long time. Without self-care and self-compassion, how can we keep our sanity when we work every day with unfathomable amounts of suffering?

It is true that we receive specialized training and are usually equipped to manage such situations with grace, but it is also true that we are humans, we have feelings, and our hearts get broken when we witness pain and suffering. We cannot go on pretending to be emotionless machines, ignoring our own heartache and anguish. We teach people how to take care of themselves and how they can nurse their wounds, it is time that we walk the talk and practice what we preach. The depths of the global pandemic placed caregivers in a tricky position, as they had the added sense of obligation to become a family for their ailing patients, many of whom ended up dying alone. That extra work came with its emotional rewards but could also continue to be a source of deep soul ache.

KEEP YOUR PRIORITIES IN PERSPECTIVE

The following are 10 ways that I think, and hope, can help caregivers navigate through the rough times:

- Safety comes first, but hope is equally important.
- Connect to yourself and your own version of a higher power.
- Connect with family and loved ones.
- Look after those in need and focus on community service.
- Advocate for, and model, calmness and inner peace.
- Find opportunities in the challenges you face. Be part of the solution, not the problem.
- Focus on emotional and spiritual needs, as those are commonly forgotten or ignored.
- Use all available resources.
- Focus on empowering the youth. Let us work toward creating a better future for our children.
- Pay extra attention to self-care and tend to your soul.

Many people with chronic health conditions were avoiding hospitals and coming to medical attention at advanced stages of their suffering. The intention of the pandemic's safety protocols was to encourage physical distancing, not to issue a social death sentence.

My patient, who died of a curable cancer because his psychosis was too severe for him to comply with chemotherapy, was the one asking the nurses how they had been and reminding them to take breaks. The day he died was very emotional for the oncology and psychiatry teams alike. People are mainly good. Humans, for the most part, are beautiful creatures, and many times their beauty shines through at the peak of their suffering or when they are literally on their deathbeds.

Because compassion fatigue HALTS (makes you Hungry, Angry, Lonely, Tired, and Scared), make sure to:
- eat healthy, and stay well hydrated;
- soothe your affect, and express your feelings;
- relate;
- talk;
- practice sleep hygiene;
- exercise;
- love yourself and your family;
- volunteer and serve; and
- leave a legacy.

There is no right or wrong way to grieve when people die under our care. There is no shame in showing distress or even shedding a tear of compassion. We need to be mindful of our professional boundaries, though, so as not to overwhelm the families of those who died. We might need to seek consultation if we want to attend, or are invited to, a patient's funeral. I have many times wished to find closure by reaching out to families of my patients to remind them of the beauty we witnessed caring for their loved ones.

We might struggle with feelings of guilt or inadequacy and start to question our competence and second-guess our decisions. We might become irritable or even angry at ourselves, our families, our patients, our coworkers, the cause of death, or the whole profession. We might feel like a failure and think of quitting. We come close to walking away on multiple occasions, but the field holds a power over us every time we are about to exit its doors. That power, I believe, is love. We love what we do, and we cannot see ourselves doing anything else as rewarding.

Four things are needed for a healthy psyche. Remember LOVE:
- forming healthy attachments and relationships (through Listening)
- expressing emotions and controlling impulses (through offering Options)
- developing a sound self-image (through Validation)
- achieving one's full potential (through Empowerment)

Regardless of how we grieve, it is important that we acknowledge and honor our emotions, and cope with them in safe and healthy ways. We have the right to be sad but not self-destructive and we have the right to be angry but without hurting others.

Here is a story to elicit not only the pain but also the joy of working with patients, and to explore how we can console our souls:

Love Heals

"Here we go again, tending to another grieving family. I dread this part of my job, and I don't remember ever signing up for it," sighed dismayed Tasha, a 24-year-old African American certified nursing assistant. She was about to enter the room of Mrs. Wilson, one of her favorite clients, who had been at the nursing home for two years and had just lost her husband to COVID-19 without being able to say goodbye to him due to the quarantine restrictions.

Tasha had always loved Mrs. Wilson, who was one of the kindest people you could ever meet and who also reminded Tasha of her own mother, who had been diagnosed with advanced dementia.

Tasha gently approached Mrs. Wilson, who was sitting in her reclining chair, and said, while handing her an assortment of roses, "I'm so sorry, Mrs. Wilson; I just heard the news. I can't imagine what it must be like to lose a spouse after 50 years."

"Oh, Tasha my dear, thank you," said Mrs. Wilson, fidgeting. "He wasn't only my husband. He was also my best friend and soul mate. I can't believe I wasn't allowed to be there holding his hands at a time he needed me the most. How can I ever live with that betrayal?"

"I'm not sure what to say, Mrs. Wilson," said Tasha, rubbing the grieving woman's hand, "But from the way you two cared for each other, I know that his heart was at peace and that he loved you until his last breath."

"I know deep down in my heart that he did and still does, but he was unable to be comforted while gasping for air. He was denied human touch when that was exactly what he needed. I'm heartbroken at the thought that he spent his last few minutes alone. That must be a horrible feeling."

"I hate this pandemic," Tasha replied. "I understand the physical distancing thing, but many people are socially dying," she added, now visibly upset.

"We're social beings, my child. We don't do well in isolation. And now with George gone, loneliness is something I need to get used to," said Mrs. Wilson, fighting back tears.

"Oh, Mrs. Wilson," said Tasha, handing her a box of tissues and again patting her hand, "It's okay to cry. We're humans after all, and it's only expected that we show emotions when we lose someone we love. I wonder if we can remember the good times too, and celebrate George's life, not only his death. And please never think that you are alone. Everybody loves you here."

"You're right, my dear. Death is only the end of life; it's not the end of the relationship." Mrs. Wilson paused reflectively, then said, "I need to redefine my relationship with George now. I know he doesn't like to see me like this, but it has been hard, really hard."

"Of course it has. That's why we encourage families of those who passed to take the time to mourn but also to remember happy memories, and not dwell on guilt," said Tasha, looking the grieving widow right in the eye as if sending her a full load of empathy. "You tried your best given the circumstances. We live in crazy times. It's important for you to find self-compassion and self-forgiveness and do acts of self-care so George's soul can rest in peace."

"Thank you, dear, you're always helpful," said Mrs. Wilson, exhaling what felt like a ball of fire from her gut. "You go home now and give your mom a big hug for me. Always appreciate those you love before they're gone. I'll be fine, I promise."

Tasha stood up and tucked her in before saying lovingly, "Good night, Mrs. Wilson, I love you, and I'll see you Monday. Don't you dare go anywhere."

"Yes, ma'am," giggled Mrs. Wilson. "I love you, too. Have a good weekend."

Tasha backed toward the door while keeping eye contact. "You do the same, Mrs. Wilson."

A few months earlier, this encounter would have had a totally different ending, as Tasha was not as aware of her own boundaries, her emotional needs, and the impact of caregiving on her soul. But now she was practicing gratitude and mindful meditation daily. She was no longer taking the burden of her work home. She smiled while exiting the nursing home, walking toward her car with the mantra repeating in her head, "I am a conduit for relief, not a receptacle for grief." She was thinking, "I can't wait for the day I return home and hug my mom and brother again."

She texted her fiancé from the motel room where she had been staying for the past several weeks because of the pandemic. "Bobby, I can't thank you enough for checking on Mom and Jamal, I love you to pieces." She then called the refugee family she had adopted in memory of her older brother, Jerome, who had died in Iraq. "Hey, Mrs. Hamdan, Tasha here. I just wanted to make sure you guys are doing okay. Please let me know if you or the kids need anything."

This story is not at all uncommon. Caregivers feel the pain of their patients. The gentler the caregiver, the more prone they are to compassion fatigue and burnout. That is why it was important for Tasha to bear witness to Mrs. Wilson's pain without internalizing it. It is a skill that she needed to master. Through self-compassion, she can now meet her own needs and be available to show up more authentically for both her clients and her loved ones.

Be kind to yourself and others. These are words of wisdom from the Center for Adolescent Studies:

- Self-compassion is one of the best tools to reduce compassion fatigue.
- Trauma can lead to negative self-attribution, mistrust of caregivers and social agencies, and expectation of future victimization.
- Adverse childhood experiences can lead to social, emotional, and cognitive impairments, then to adoption of health-risky behaviors, then to disease and disability, then to early death.
- Have a bidirectional relationship between internal and interpersonal attunement. When you attune to yourself, it makes it easier for you to attune to your clients and those under your care.
- Deep listening: This does not involve a solution-focused mode but, rather, sitting with and bearing witness. A relationally corrective experience from a caring fellow human who gives the clients time and respect so they can feel seen, heard, felt, and witnessed. That leads to trust, comfort, and more sharing in an authentic relationship.
- Deep listening leads to understanding, empathy, compassion, and connection.

Healing by Focusing on Beauty and Joy

Beauty is an essential ingredient for healing, not only in a medical context but in all human interactions. Our interpersonal spaces can and should always be places of safety, hope, and beauty. Going through the Harvard Program in Refugee Trauma, I had the joy of spending two weeks immersed in the beauty of Italy. We mingled and dined with the locals and enjoyed our four-hour-long meals. As a caregiver, it is important that you pause to look with awe at the mesmerizing beauty all around you.

According to Michael Hollifield, MD, the 12 steps in the path toward whole health are:

1. Define what you live for.
2. Be here now.
3. Imagine your highest self.
4. Identify things lost. Regain what you can and mourn the rest.
5. Nourish and work your body.
6. Expand your comfort zones.
7. Connect with social structures.
8. Reject negative statements about yourself and the world.
9. Rethink trauma.

10. Forgive yourself.
11. Find and maintain joy.
12. Teach.

"Practice beauty," Dr. Mollica taught me:

> Art is the true revolution of the human spirit. We find one
> another in beauty. Beautiful words create beautiful worlds,
> and beautiful actions restore faith in humanity. Beauty is
> expressed in how we welcome and care for each other, how we
> move without fear into each other's embrace. When the sunrise
> and sunset do not evoke feelings in us anymore, it means our
> souls are sick.

His words of wisdom resonated deeply with me. "Omar, if you are
not looking for beauty in every encounter, then you are not practicing medicine."

"Kidnapped by the current fast-paced, self-centered, individualistic,
and demanding lifestyle, societies have forgotten how to float with the
admiration, kindness, and curiosity that they once carried," he added.
Heavy caseloads, long working hours, and the nonstop demands and
pressures placed on us take away from our capacity to appreciate, enjoy,
receive, and give beauty.

Our relationships are both anchors and lighthouses in a dark, storm-
ridden sea. See yourself in the people you serve. Do things with, not
for, them. Shift from a hierarchical to a collaborative approach. Your
client is the subject-matter expert on their life experiences and their
needs. The most predictive factor for resilience is social belonging, and
what we need most right now is human connection.

"Healing takes imagination, not only resources," argued Mollica;

"There is no healing without beauty. The healing space is about two empathic people who can co-construct a meaning and build a new worldview." Seek beauty in others and look for beauty in everything.

You might find beauty in the least expected places. I remember a patient who I thought was racist because of the way he looked. When I first met him, he was reading a book by Rumi, and as he shared the quote "There are beautiful things that you can only see in the dark." We reflected on that together and ended up co-crafting a beautiful therapeutic relationship.

When to Ask for Professional Help

These are some of the red flags of burnout that might mean you need referral to specialized services:

- strong somatic symptoms, like severe pains, relentless migraines, and non-epileptic seizures
- psychotic symptoms, like delusions and hallucinations
- not looking after your basic needs
- inability to function at baseline or neglecting activities of daily living (ADLs)
- unhealthy sleep habits
- engagement in impulsive and risky behaviors
- suicidal thoughts, especially with access to lethal means
- violence
- use of alcohol and illicit drugs

Needing to lean on professional assistance is not a reason for judgment or despair. Do not get discouraged. Never see that as a sign of weakness; rather, it is a sign of courage. It would help if the culture promoted self-care. There was a time when caregivers were required or highly encouraged to engage in therapy themselves. I admire colleagues who are open about their feelings. They know how to share them without overwhelming the listener, and they reach out to all available social and professional resources in their immediate environment and in the community because they know that healers who heal themselves are better able to help others heal.

I would like to conclude this section with Smink (2018) reminding us that "Compassion fatigue occurs because you care. It is depleting because it requires inner discipline of heroic proportions. Healing from it is like a train ride, so take your time, do not rush, hop on and off."

Reflection Corner

Welcome to this sacred space. This is a breathing room. It is for you to pause and reflect in if you wish to do so.

Thank you for your service.

You have seen the impact on your soul of working with clients and their loved ones.

Take your time to heal from the pain of interacting with the last patient so you can find the joy in caring for the next.

I invite you now to do something kind to your body, like:
- Eat a healthy snack.
- Drink a cup of water.
- Take a nap.
- Stretch.
- Breathe.
- Enjoy the outdoors.

2 / The Healing Power of Family

The Impact of Caregiver Fatigue on Family

In a healthy family context, family members are like body organs. If one organ is injured, the whole body feels that pain. Trauma can shake the foundation of the family unit. It is therefore crucial that the family stand united when traumatized. Trauma can make, rather than break, a family that speaks up and invests in healing.

But when a family, for whatever reason, is unable to engage in the work of healing, trauma can force family members to see one another as enemies. Here is a story to illustrate how trauma can threaten the very existence of the family system.

Abandoned

"Hey there, this is Arjun with the Sacred Valley Hospital here in Oregon. I'm trying to reach Joshua, please."

"This is Josh speaking. What's this about?"

"Hey, Mr. Butler. I'm one of the nurse aides caring for your sister Joy. She's been admitted to the intensive care unit and she's in bad shape. I thought you guys might want to know. Do you think you might be able to come see her? I know you live in another state, but she would love to see you. It's her wish, maybe her last. I'm afraid she has only a few days to live."

"Oh my, I'm sorry to hear that. What's wrong with her this time?"

"She has endocarditis—heart infection, that is—and her heart is failing."

"Oh, she likely got that from her IV drug use. That's why the family decided to have nothing to do with her. I don't think anyone will be coming down there, to be honest. I'm sorry, I know that sounds bad, but her substance use has caused all kinds of damage. She burned all her bridges with the rest of the family; I'm the only one who still keeps in touch with her."

"I understand, and I'll respect whatever decision the family makes. We'll care for her to the best of our ability and make sure she doesn't die alone. It's just that we can never replace a family."

"Let me talk to my parents and get back to you. Just don't count on anyone being there in person. I have my own struggles, but I'll speak with her through video if she's able to talk."

"Thank you, Josh, that would be really wonderful."

Arjun hung up and went to check on Joy.

"They aren't coming, right?" she asked.

"Well, Ms. Butler, I was able to get hold of your brother Josh. He said he'll be talking to your folks. He'd love to see you through video. If tonight works for you, I can arrange that."

"Yes, please, Arjun, you're so sweet. Josh is the only one who found a space in his heart for forgiveness. He struggled with addiction too. I would really love to see him and also be able to talk to Mom and Dad. I need to make amends and tell them how sorry I am. I know I screwed up, and I know they're mad at me, but I'm really sorry, really I am." She was now sobbing.

"Please don't stress out, Joy, your heart can't handle more pain. I hope they'll be ready to reach out to you, but don't be disappointed if they're not. I'll for sure keep trying. We're your family here, everybody loves you. Let me get going now on the video conference with Josh."

"Thank you, Arj, you're the best," Joy exclaimed, both excited and exhausted.

Arjun was a 29-year-old nurse aide who had recently immigrated to the United States from India. Coming from a large family, he wondered how a family could "abandon" one of its members. Was it a cultural norm or a moral failure? he asked himself.

Being part of a pool of float staff, he sometimes got assigned to the inpatient psychiatric unit. He had always been amazed at the wide spectrum of family dynamics he witnessed coming into play between the clients and their loved ones. For a small minority, families were overprotective and intrusive and tended to hover like a helicopter over all the details of the patient's experience and every aspect of the treatment plan. For the lucky few, families were quite involved and supportive but appropriately so, maintaining healthy boundaries and encouraging empowerment and self-efficacy. Most of his patients, however, went through the scary experience of inpatient psychiatric hospitalization alone; they neither viewed their family system as a protective factor nor considered it a source of solace and strength during times of crisis.

So, what makes families abandon their loved one at a time when they were needed the most? He wondered if he should look with compassion at both parties and try to help encourage rebuilding bridges and healing past trauma.

When he asked his patients about the reason(s) why they had no one to turn to for support, they came up with many explanations, ranging from self-loathing and blaming everything on something they had done wrong, to lashing out, accusing the whole world of being unfair to them, and taking no ownership of their share in the damage done to the relationship or of their responsibility to try to repair it.

Mental illness is a very lonely and alienating experience, even with support. To have a family that cares makes all the difference. To see visitors walk through the doors of the hospital to show unconditional love and acceptance to their loved ones and meet them where they were was something that warmed his heart every single time.

He wondered if there were really any legitimate excuses for our giving up on each other. Was it okay to accept family breakdown and dysfunction as the status quo and the norm? Were people really burning bridges when they had active symptoms of mental illness or addiction? Was there ever room for healing and family bonding when things "hit rock bottom"? Could we see the trauma story, not our loved one, as the enemy? And could we view the trauma we endured as the reason for resilience and strength of the family unit, rather than allowing it to be the source of fires that destroyed our homes?

But when betrayal, broken promises, or violence were part of the patient's legacy and history, why would a family be expected to embrace that person with open arms, just because they were now homeless, psychotic, or suicidal?

Arjun sighed and said to himself, "I'm acutely aware of the fact that healing can't be forced or expedited, and that people don't have to forgive if they aren't ready to do so. I'm just wondering if I can remind families that we engaged in a sacred contract the minute we held our children in our arms and made that very first eye contact; that promise was, I'll love, accept, defend, and be there for you unconditionally and always, no matter what. That little child is still there, under all the layers of pain and suffering and behind all the confusing labels, waiting to be found, held, and comforted. When we dig deep and find our loved ones, they'll shine. We all deserve that second or hundredth chance, even if we've messed up over and over again." He sighed again, hoping Josh would come through for his sister, and praying that Joy's parents would find room for grace so their daughter could end her ugly life in a beautiful death. "I can't wait to get home to call my family." Arjun smiled, with a heavy heart that was full of pain and joy.

Trauma that happens in a family context can terrorize and can leave ruin and wreckage behind. The family then has a decision to make: either to stand united to rebuild, or to have the trauma wipe out their home and permanently disfigure or sever family ties.

Because trauma is a family affair, it is important for traumatized caregivers to pay special attention to their loved ones. Encounters like Joy's story might make healers reflect on their own family dynamics. For Arjun, that means being intentional in how he shows gratitude and appreciation for his family even if they are thousands of miles away.

According to Smink (2018), we heal when we trust, talk, and share our feelings. That is true for the systems we work with, but it is also true in a family context. If you are a caregiver who shuts down because you do not want to "burden" your loved ones, know that your silence and emotional isolation are the burden that weighs heavily on them. Sharing your load will likely lighten theirs.

Families Are Essential for Caregivers

Caregivers do not live in a bubble; they are impacted by all the drama and trauma of this day and age. After long and depleting work hours, they sometimes go home to more emotionally taxing tasks.

Family should be empowered as the first line of defense against the impacts of trauma on caregivers. This is an important theme that is very near and dear to my heart. Healthy family dynamics provide the best shield against walking the dark paths of dysfunction and the blazing fires of destruction caused by trauma.

Family means different things to different people. For the sake of this book, I am talking about "blood family." But why am I writing about family trauma in a book about healing caregivers? The answer is that family can make or break a child (or an adult, for that matter), and trauma can make or break a family.

I had the privilege of caring for three sisters who had been sexually violated by their own father. They had endured the same trauma, but they experienced it very differently. The oldest chose denial and went on to embrace a lifestyle of strict dieting and strenuous exercise. The youngest became overprotective of her father and dissociated frequently, going into brief psychotic episodes with every flashback or nightmare about what had happened. But the middle sister chose to engage in deep and cleansing trauma work and became more able to function relatively normally and start her own small family. Incest is a horrific wound; children feel trapped because "the monster never leaves; it comes out of the closet every night." It is heartbreaking when parents are predators.

I keep repeating that most wounds happen relationally, and healing therefore mostly needs to take place in a relational context. One of the most complex relationships is that between family members.

My wife was recently at a restaurant with one of her best friends. They noticed a woman sitting alone at a corner table. My wife wanted to invite her over, but her friend said they should not intrude. The woman came over to their table and asked if they spoke Arabic, and then shared how much she enjoyed traveling, visiting different countries, and meeting new people. They asked her if she was waiting for someone, and she said that she used to have a weekly dinner with her son at that exact place, but he had recently passed away. This was her first time coming back to the restaurant since his passing; she had come to keep his memory alive. My wife's friend told her that they had noticed her deep sadness even before she spoke, and that they had even wondered if they should invite her over. The grieving mother said, "I wish you had. I would have really loved it." That was a reminder of the importance of deep kindness and how a random small act of compassion toward a total stranger can brighten their day. It was also an important lesson that a loss in a family context can shatter our hearts into a million pieces, but we can always make the choice to celebrate our loved ones and keep their legacy alive.

I expand on how family can cope with trauma in Resources 2.1 and 2.2, which provide tools we can use to bond with our loved ones, especially after trauma. Resource 2.1, *House of Joy*, offers tips to help caregivers bond with their families. Simple acts of kindness, like smiling, safe touch, and eye contact, can go a long way in bonding healers with their loved ones. Resource 2.2, *This is Us, Together*, is a declaration that helps traumatized families acknowledge and address their trauma in a united front.

When I get home, I sit in the driveway for a couple of minutes to unwind, breathe, and center myself before I am ready to be with my family. A house feels like home because of the dynamics among family members. I make the conscious choice of leaving the stress from work in front of the garage, because I want to delight in my loved ones and enjoy our time together. Sometimes I pretend that I am running out of energy so my daughters can jump on me and recharge my battery with their hugs. We all find joy in that exercise. I want them to remember that I will always try my best to be a safe father. If you like the sound of this activity, give it a try.

Most of us can see and appreciate how central the role of a family is, yet some caregivers avoid their families, for many complicated reasons. I listened with awe as I recorded stories of caregivers who had to stay away from family during the height of the COVID-19 pandemic for fear of infecting them; spouses who got into custody battles to "protect" their children from the caregiving parent; staff who were unable to hug or touch their loved ones for several weeks or months on end; caregivers inside COVID units basically living behind locked doors in total isolation; staff with traumatic memories that got activated by the pandemic; and caregivers engaging in unhealthy coping, like social withdrawal, addiction, domestic violence, suicide, family breakdown, and complete disconnection from support networks and their authentic self.

Self-care is essential to better serving our clients and our families. Take care of yourself and your trauma so you can take better care of your loved ones. I enjoy spending quality time with my family. One bonding exercise, available online, that we enjoy as a family is painting a picture of a human, a tree, and a house. We do that as a family and then have a discussion about what *exposure, protection*, and *nurturing* mean in a family context. The activity goes something like this:

- Human: Feet (what anchors us?), body (what represents our core?), hands (what are some ways we can contribute?)
- Tree: This is our family tree. What makes our roots as a family? What do the trunk and the branches represent? What about the fruits we produce?
- House: What makes our foundation? How about the walls (pillars) and our roof?

Exposure (what trauma happened to our family?), protection (what helps shield us from that exposure?), and nurturing (what are things that nourish and sustain us as a traumatized family?), are some of the themes we cover during this fun, yet healing, family-bonding activity.

Self-awareness is another tool for avoiding the spread of toxic stress. I remember once reading that "Mean words are like weapons that children store and can later use to hurt themselves or others." I asked a group of youth what their favorite animal was. Some shared that they felt like fish because when they cried nobody seemed to notice, others wanted to become birds so they could fly away, and others wished to be turtles or baby kangaroos so they could hide when their parents fought or when their small or big worlds became unsafe. You would never use abusive language toward your supervisors, your clients, or toward strangers for that matter, so why talk to your loved ones in a toxic way? Children should always be viewed as part of the solution, not only as part of the problem. If you are wounded, try to nurse your wounds. If you had a rough day at work, do not take it out on your family.

Listening and appreciation are important in the family context.

Trauma can happen to any family, regardless of their personal or generational history with adversity. My family's encounters with death and violence were many, like losing a sister to brain cancer, a nephew to violent extremism, and a mother to advanced dementia and liver failure. All these encounters made me more vocal about taking advantage of the current moment and appreciating loved ones before it is too late. My book *Untangled* (2019) dives deeper into these topics and can serve as a guide for bonding and healing the family unit. Family is the building block of society. Healthy families make healthy societies.

You do not have to go through war to get traumatized. For caregivers, our frontlines feel like a permanent war zone. Trauma is ugly; it can rip apart family ties and threaten to destroy the family unit. Given my distance from Libya for over a decade, I am in a better position to continue to have strong relationships with all my siblings and relatives despite their diverse political viewpoints. I am very close to my brother in Egypt, who is unable to enter Libya because of his political views. It is something that my beloved mother always taught me; until her last breath she kept saying, "If you love me, take care of each other and love one another."

It is common for parents to become depleted and even disgruntled. What can you do to be loving at those times when your fuse is short? Here are some suggestions:

- Let your kids recharge you through mutual nourishment. It is easy to think as parents that we are the only ones who should give emotional nourishment, but it can be mutual. Our children can nourish us if we allow it. I never advise or advocate for a child to be the sole source of nurturing for their parents; rather, both are part of the healing exchange.
- Pause to take care of yourself. Close your eyes. Breathe deep. Drink some water. Take a five-minute walk in the fresh air.

Listen to some comedy. Take a nap. Pray. Use kind self-talk. Brain surgeons, airplane pilots, and train conductors take breaks, so why do not you? Your job is more delicate than theirs.

Some parents have many things on their plate. But remember that you do not have to do everything for everyone right now. There are things on your list that you can delay or delegate.

You deal with a malleable and potentially fragile psyche. You mold and build a human. Take that very seriously.

- Leave your work problems at work. Make a conscious decision to leave any job-related issues out of the house, and vice versa.

- Wait to go online until after you spend quality time with your children, or, even better, do it after they go to bed. Remember the value of sleep as a self-care tool.

Appreciating Our Partners

There are other people and many resources to help get the job done. We need to stop believing and behaving as if we are the center of the universe. The world will not crumble if we catch a little rest.

The sacred contract:
- Home is a place of safety, and a source of peace for the body, mind, heart, and soul.
- The best parents are those best to their family.
- Domestic violence, in any form, is a dishonorable act.
- A relationship is a partnership. A plane needs both wings to fly and land safely.

- Marriage is a journey full of sacrifices and compromises, tears, headaches, and heartache, but also full of joy. Be invested and be deliberate. It takes hard work and commitment to improve and heal your marriage.
- It takes two to tangle, and two to untangle.
- Relationship is about connection, not perfection.
- If you focus on the positive in your partner, you will find plenty of it.
- No one is perfect. Love your spouse unconditionally.
- One of the best things you can do for your children is to love their other parent.
- A conflict is to be viewed as an opportunity to learn and grow closer, rather than an excuse to insult and defame your partner.

Spouses should treat each other with grace. I am a strong believer that one of the best things you can do for your children is to love their other parent, or at least treat them with respect and civility, even if there has been trauma in the relationship. Children need the safety of the family umbrella, especially during stormy weather. Unfortunately, many times that is not the case. Marital discord and domestic violence confuse the psyche and make children blame themselves and engage in self-loathing language and even self-destructive behaviors.

Let your family know that you always appreciate them. Let us frequently tell our loved ones how

Marriage is a sacred contract that is based on the foundations of love and mercy. Unfortunately, however, many households struggle with the dysfunctional dynamics of emotional distancing, marital discord, extramarital affairs, and interpersonal chaos. We must turn our homes into places of safety, peace, hope, affection, and tranquility.

joyful and honored we are to have them in our life. Humans thrive when adored. Offering external validation is an art we need to master to fill the emotional tanks of our loved ones and fulfill their basic needs for love and affection.

If you want to be treated like royalty, treat your partner that way, and if you want an angel as a spouse, turn your home into a garden, for angels belong in paradise, not hell.

Practice mindfulness with family. Mindfulness is a beautiful gift that you can share with your loved ones. Mindfulness, according to the Center for Adolescent Studies, is

> the present moment awareness with an attitude of non-reactivity, noticing what is around us and our internal state, without judgment. It is not about being calm but finding ways to center oneself regardless of one's emotional state. It is the capacity to have inner peace despite the outer chaos. You do not have to be actively meditating to practice mindfulness. Rather, master gentle moments of pause to tune in to what is authentic to you.

I use play- and art-therapy techniques to teach my loved ones how to meditate and be mindful, such as "Smell the roses, blow the candles," or using bubbles or balloons to master breathing exercises. Also helpful are stress balls and soothing lotions and aromas. Connect with nature, play with sand; use whatever resources are at your disposal.

Share your stories and listen to theirs. That is another way family gets nurtured. Show vulnerability, normalize the experience of struggling during times of distress, and demonstrate the importance of self-care to continue to be the best nurturer you can be for yourself and everyone around you. Children look up to us for guidance when they are faced with big feelings. The thing they will likely remember most about trauma is how their family coped with it. We need to model ourselves showing vulnerability so they see us as humans who will inevitably cause ruptures in the relationship but who will quickly try to repair any damage. To that end, it does not take away from our dignity as parents to admit fault or apologize when we mess up, because we surely will.

Tend to Your Children by Bonding With Them

You might be tired, lethargic, unmotivated, and neglecting self-care. When we are exhausted, like after being on call on a busy night or after a long and stressful day at work, we might not be emotionally available to be at our best for our loved ones. Rethink your central role in your family and tend to your soul. Traumatic and stressful events can impact the nature and the quality of attachment and can cast dark shadows on the relationship.

Develop resilience and model it for your children. Parents' self-care and resilience, or lack thereof, greatly influence how well their children cope. Being intentional in relationships can help one manage challenging experiences. As caregivers, we need to remember that our children are watching, they learn through following our example. During difficult times, we need to normalize and model practicing self-care at the individual, family, and community levels. It is also important to take the time to try to answer your children's questions, because otherwise they will look for the answers somewhere else.

You are the most important person in your child's life; let that sink in. Knowing that charity starts at home, I decided to learn to focus on my own children, even though my heart sinks every time I leave behind traumatized children in a refugee camp or war zone. I now try to help these causes through training, supervision, and consultation from a distance.

Children's attachment

Attachment is how children and their caregivers bond. We are our children's rocks and anchors. When they feel bonded with an emotionally available parent or caregiver, they feel safer. No matter what happens, they feel attached to someone who is genuinely trying their best to take care of them.

Children who do not feel attached will feel unsafe and on their own. They might then search for someone else they can bond with, often anyone who gives them attention. This can send them from one person to the next in a desperate search for an anchor, jeopardizing their safety in the process. We hear stories daily of children who run away from abusive or neglectful homes, or even from homes that are seemingly healthy, chasing a mirage, something and anything that could fill that void in their hearts. These children risk engaging in self-destructive habits like substance use or sexualized behaviors, potentially leading to trauma from run-ins with human traffickers and other dangerous groups, dark ideologies, and toxic relationships.

Attachment also makes it possible for children to withstand bullies and predators, because they feel secure in the bond with their caregivers. Attachment becomes their shielding armor.

Types of family attachment styles

There are four major types of attachment styles, according to John Bowlby:

- Secure—often displayed by children who have structure in their daily lives and who feel unconditionally loved. They might feel somewhat anxious when their parent is absent but are quickly comforted when the parent returns.
- Avoidant—often displayed by abused children. They do not easily make eye contact and will feel safer when the parent is away. That sounds incredibly sad, does it not?

- Ambivalent—often displayed by children who are neglected. Whether or not the parent is there does not really matter because the parent's absence and presence are equally insignificant. Heartbreaking, is it not?
- Disorganized—often displayed by children who get mixed messages from their caregiver. The parent goes back and forth between acting loving and abusive, confusing the child, who becomes perplexed, feeling both cared for and threatened.

These four attachment styles are also the four parenting styles. Secure children are usually the result of parents with a secure parenting style. We often adopt the parenting style of our parents because it is all that we know, but that is not always the best approach. The good news is that you can improve your parenting style, starting now. Begin by saying you want to raise secure children, and then commit to making one small positive change at a time, being invested, and being consistent.

Provide bonding time and attention to encourage secure attachment. Children deserve to have their need for attachment met. Parents need to learn how to attach so their children and families can feel safe to bond. Be around your loved ones in a relaxed way. If you always display restlessness and negative energy, your children will start to make excuses to avoid you. It is a shame when our children feel they need to walk on eggshells around us. If your child shuts down when you enter the house and relaxes when you exit, then you need to urgently and immediately examine your priorities and commit to change. See which of your basic needs is not being met, and then fill your tank.

Be a warm presence in your child's life. We show a consistently warm presence to prove to our children that despite the world's dark side, and despite their own feelings of worthlessness, they can experience beauty, healing, and joy. By *warm presence* I mean that our children find us welcoming, supportive, and there for them, regardless. We are reliably in their corner, thinking the best of them and giving our best to them. You do not have to necessarily spend money to bond with your children; what matters is being safe and available.

I was blessed during the COVID-19 pandemic quarantine season to create a YouTube channel with my three children. We called it the Daughter-Father Bonding (DFB) project. Through short educational videos, we have attempted to give practical tips to strengthen the relationship between children and their parents. It was quite a powerful bonding exercise for all of us. If you are looking for simple and fun ways to bond with the little ones under your roof, check us out.

How to improve your attachment with your child:
- Create a safe space for both the body and the spirit.
- Make eye contact.
- Be a warm presence and offer comfort.
- Accept and validate your child's feelings.
- Spend time together, one-on-one, without excessive technology or distractions.
- Talk together with an open-door policy.
- Speak well of your child.
- Protect your child from outside harm as best you can.
- Discipline without violence, shaming, or withholding forgiveness.
- Learn the art of smiling.

Interact With Your Family
to Gain Their Cooperation

You do not have to threaten your children to get them to cooperate. Spending time together would likely be a better approach. A time-in will win over a time-out any day. A time-in means to attune to your child through spending time with them at their moments of distress. I have tried the time-in technique on many occasions, and it works like a charm every single time.

It is neither the punishment nor the reward that really has the long-lasting impact, but rather the genuine validation of our children's feelings and experiences, and the empathic stance toward their struggles. Traumatized children might not have the "right" words to describe their experience. They will then try to get our attention with behaviors. If we punish or shame emotional expression, they will learn not to trust their feelings and not to speak up in the future.

Build trust and avoid micromanaging. Parents need to build trust for children to become motivated to act responsibly. It is important to connect with the children before directing them. The shortest way to someone's head is through their heart. Parents should adjust to switching from a "micromanager" role to a more child-empowering "consultant" role. When you see your children struggling to figure out the world, empathize, allow space, encourage, and observe. You can always intervene if things get unsafe. Parenting is a journey, so fill your tank, be in the driver's seat, and enjoy the scenery, but watch out for dangerous road conditions.

Here are a few words of wisdom from the Center for Adolescent Studies to help you bond with your children:

- Build age-appropriate dialogue: Acts (doing) are more assuring than words (talking) in younger kids. Older children respond to words of assurance. Anticipate, accept, and respond to the needs of your children.

- Stay calm, connect through empathizing with the feeling, and engage in collaborative problem-solving. Accepting the feeling does not mean condoning the behavior. You need to be flexible but also set limits. You do not need to be your children's friend but strive to be a friendly parent.

- Focus on safety, reassurance, and consistency, provide brief concrete information, limit media and adult conversations, and filter the world for them so they do not get overwhelmed or overstimulated. Model coping, either implicitly, such as by allowing them to see you practice deep breathing; or explicitly, such as by telling them, "I'm going on a walk to calm myself down."

Use simple explanations. During stressful times, children appreciate simple language about how they can stay safe and how they can contribute to the safety of others. During big times, like a global pandemic, our children will certainly ask big questions and will try to wrestle with big feelings. Always invite and welcome questions and interactive discussions, involve and empower them, make them part of the solution, and answer their questions the best you can. Remember that if you dismiss dialogue or shut down conversations, it will be difficult for bridges of trust to be built. Trust and safety are foundational in our homes, and open channels of communication seem to help bond and heal families, even those with severe trauma.

Meet your own needs so you can meet your children's needs. Caregivers' basic needs must be met if they are expected to fill emotional voids for their children. An invested parent, even if through the help of a caring professional, could fill their own emotional buckets and move from being discouraged to being delighted in the child and the relationship. When caregivers see self-care as a responsibility toward their loved ones, they will feel better about having something left in them to share, and the children in turn will notice and welcome the new energy—a win-win situation. In a family context, there should be no losers.

Healing in a Family Context

Burnout can affect our families as well as ourselves. It is not easy to love or be married to a caregiver. Those who love us need to know the different ways we give and receive love; they need to learn our love language and realize that we might give and receive love differently at different times. Burnout can impact our capacity to accept and offer love. Burnout can sound like this:

- "I wall myself off, I feel alone, I'm tired, I'm banged up, I'm beaten up, my body hurts, I'm mostly sad or numb, and I get frustrated easily."
- "I put a lot of myself into caring, and sometimes I judge myself harshly if I'm not perfect at it."
- "I need to retreat to my cave for a while, and I won't have any guests over."

Trauma Is a Family Affair

Trauma can affect the entire family. Not every traumatized family is ready to open a discussion about healing, but for those that are, it could be a deeply cleansing experience for all involved.

I remember one patient admitted under my care, an elderly gentleman who had been found in his car during a snowstorm, confused and almost frozen to death. We treated his delirium and dementia, and although his cognition improved, he still could not remember anything about his family. We went through his cell phone contacts and called a few people, who said that he had one daughter, on the other side of the country. With permission from the hospital leadership, I contacted her on social media. She was very excited to learn that her father, who she had not heard from in 10 years, was still alive. They had severed ties over his heavy drinking. The family ended up flying him out to live with them. It was a beautiful reunion. Sometimes the remedy is not a medication, but a dose of affection and family bonding. A family has the power to heal its members. As a physician, when all other measures fail, I prescribe hope. As a caregiver, I urge you to tend to your family.

I would also argue that trauma is like a cancer. Untreated, it can quickly spread throughout the body, leading to serious, malignant, and even fatal consequences.

My wife had to watch in horror the bloody civil war in Libya, a country she loved but had never set foot in. With heavy heart, she gave me her permission and blessings, time after time, so I could go and serve, leaving her and three beautiful and very young children behind. She had to experience her own PTSD fearing that her husband, who she viewed as a superhero, might never be around to care for his small family. But I needed to go and tend to my parents. What could she have done differently, and what else could I have done?

The impact of trauma on survivors is a heavily studied and researched topic in the scientific literature. There is great deal of focus on the individualistic (client-centered) interventions that encourage acknowledging the personal narrative, commonly referred to as the trauma story. Trauma, however, deeply affects family dynamics. Trauma is more than just PTSD. When a family member gets traumatized either because

The Lord is my shepherd; I shall not want.
He maketh me to lie down in green pastures:
He leadeth me beside the still waters.

He restoreth my soul: He leadeth me in the
paths of righteousness for His name's sake.

Yea, though I walk through the valley of
the shadow of death, I will fear no evil: for
thou art with me; thy rod and thy staff
they comfort me.

Thou preparest a table before me in the
presence of mine enemies: thou anointest
my head with oil; my cup runneth over.

Surely goodness and mercy shall follow me
all the days of my life: and I will dwell in
the house of the Lord for ever.

-Psalms 23

of abuse, neglect, or a natural or man-made disaster, or through inter-personal violence or bearing witness to suffering, their core beliefs and deep-seated foundations of safety and trust might get shattered, impacting their interactions with the rest of the family. Trauma survivors then might internalize their experiences and withdraw, becoming depressed, anxious, or even suicidal; or might externalize them and become irritable, angry, hostile, violent, or even homicidal. Family members are the easy target for our displaced and projected emotions, especially anger. We tend to take our frustration out on our loved ones. A traumatized parent can pass their anxiety on to the children and become overprotective or even suffocating, limiting the child's full potential and preventing them from discovering the beautiful things the world can offer them and the more beautiful things they can offer the world, leading to resentment on the part of the child. Or a traumatized parent can lash out, repeating the dysfunctional cycle of violence and using hurtful words and actions that cause children to doubt their beauty and question their self-worth. A traumatized parent needs to work diligently through their issues and confront their shadows so they can eventually break free from the shackles of trauma and connect with their families in healthy and empowering ways.

Healing is not only working with clients and systems but also tending to ourselves and the people we love. Here is a story to illustrate that:

Breaking Through

"Dr. Baker, this is Elizabeth with human resources."

"Hey, Liz, good to hear from you. What can I do for you? Is everything okay?"

"It's about Grace—Dr. Chen. A family filed a complaint.

Dr. Chen overlooked a critical lab, and the patient ended up in the ICU needing intubation. Fortunately, she survived."

"Oh, that's good that there was no permanent damage. Give me the patient's info and a few days so I can review the case and talk to Grace."

Later in the week, he and Grace met in his office.

"There isn't much I can do at this point, Grace. HR wanted to open an investigation about what happened to Ms. Robins."

"What do you mean there's nothing you can do, Dan?" Grace replied, irritated. "You're my supervisor, and I expect to count on your support. And it's a case review, not an investigation, Dan. I'm not some kind of criminal. I hate this. We care for tens of thousands of people, and the minute we overlook a minor detail or make one small mistake we get called into HR and hear threats about reporting us to the medical board. It seems like the system only notices us when there's an issue, and then we get viewed as impaired physicians in need of rehabilitation. When was the last time you called me into your office to give a compliment or share some positive feedback? I'm tired, Dan. Very tired. This isn't worth it. There're other places that'll treat me better."

"I agree with your sentiment, Grace, and I'm so sorry if I sounded unsupportive or if you felt disrespected. That's not my intention at all; you know that's not my style, and you know how much I value and appreciate you. It's just that my hands get tied whenever HR and administration gets involved. I'm tired too, Grace. We, primary care physicians, are treated like factory workers. I see at least 25 patients every day in addition to all my other administrative duties. Not enough time to even know most of the folks I'm supposed to care for. It's taking its toll on my soul."

"Not only on us, Dan," Grace replied, now on the verge of tears. "I'm taking my stress out on my girl. She's an only child and is only 15. She doesn't deserve this. It's unfair. I'm a single parent, but I'll choose my family over work any day. I'll deal with HR later. I'd really like to get going now."

Grace exited the office and called her daughter, Claire. "Hey, sweetheart, it's Friday afternoon. Are you up for having a fun weekend?"

Claire, suspicious, hesitated. "Hmm, well, what do you have in mind, Mom?"

"Let's head to the beach. Spend the whole weekend there. The weather is supposed to be gorgeous. We'll come home Sunday evening. I just miss you. It's been so long since we had an alone bonding time. What do you say?"

"Sure, Mom, I'd really like that. But can you please not be on your laptop the whole time?"

"Well, guess what, the computer is staying home. Maybe you can stay away from your phone, too."

"You've got a deal," Claire laughed, now excited about the new energy in the relationship.

Grace was able to find grace for her issues at work. She made the decision to disengage, and to instead deliberately prioritize self-care and her relationship with her daughter. Healthy caregivers know when to be assertive and take active measures to respect their boundaries and protect their loved ones.

Our family deserves our care. Our loved ones do not deserve anything less than every single ounce of our healing love and tender care. When our needs as caregivers are met, we become better parents and have more capacity to dispense affection and joy. We and our loved ones flourish together as a loving family. Togetherness is the foundation of the family unit. Together, we heal, and together we blossom.

In Resource 2.1, *House of Joy*, and Resource 2.2, *This Is Us, Together*, I cover more of this topic, hoping that helps traumatized families honor their trauma story and use these tools as a guide on their journey toward healing.

If trauma survivors and their loved ones are left uneducated about the root causes and the effects of sudden and dramatic changes in thinking styles, emotional responses, and behavioral reactions, then trauma can come between family members and threaten the very existence of the family unit. Many family structures do corrode, crumble, dissolve, or permanently vanish because of trauma. Do not let that happen to you.

Trauma should be viewed by family members as the common enemy and the challenge they need to tackle together. It should not rob them of their joy or destroy their bond. This is easier said than done, though. We need to invest in training traumatized families and equipping them with the skills they need to do that.

I remember someone coming to me after a talk I gave about honoring marriage as a sacred contract and loving your partner. He said that on the way to the lecture he had a big fight with his wife and that they were seriously considering divorce. Never underestimate the impact of your kind words.

But how to love when you yourself feel unloved? Like many parents, you may be running on empty. By that, I mean your own buckets of safety, love, and attention may not have been filled by your parents when you were young, despite their best efforts to care for you, given their circumstances. It takes lots of self-discipline not to repeat the dysfunctional cycles.

My father was raised an orphan even though his parents were both alive. They divorced and he had to grow up with different family members, never able to make sense of the experience of being abandoned, and never having his emotional tank filled. He made sure, however, not to do the same to his own children and instead committed to being an emotionally generous and available father.

WHAT PARENTS NEED

All people have needs that must be met. These include:

- physical needs, like food and shelter
- intellectual stimulation
- social contact
- emotional connection
- spiritual satisfaction

Parents need all of this, and more:

- parental training and guidance
- healing from their own trauma
- support and input
- inspiration and aspiration
- healthy habits
- interests and hobbies
- optimism
- forgiveness, especially self-forgiveness

It is possible that your emotional needs were unfulfilled, ignored, dismissed, neglected, or even abused. How can you break the cycle of trauma and give love when you yourself feel unloved? Can you give what you have not received? Here are a few suggestions:

- Talk nicer to yourself. Positive self-dialogue lets us talk to ourselves with the love we needed to hear when we were children.
  - "Nice work being patient with the kids today."
  - "I can do this."
  - "I'm getting better at being a positive parent."

- Treat your body with tender loving care. We parent better when we feel better, and the way to feel better is to treat our bodies, minds, hearts, and souls with the love and respect they deserve. Plus, it teaches our children how to do it. Many caregivers neglect their health and ignore red flags that urge them to take breaks. It is important that you:
  - Insert one more healthy eating habit into your day.
  - Move a few extra minutes in a way that feels good. Stretch, walk, or run.
  - Sleep well, so you can recover and be ready to meet the next day refreshed. I cannot emphasize enough the importance of sleep hygiene.

- Improve how you cope. Coping skills can be learned. How you cope determines the quality of your life and how well you can love yourself and lead your family to healing from trauma.
  - Smile.
  - Praise more than you complain.
  - Listen.
  - Reach out rather than lash out.

Given that, many times, we do not do the best job reaching out to others at our time of need, we should find companionship that reaches in to hold and accept us. In the words of Bruce Perry (2021), "We are continually scanning the relational environment for signs of approval and belonging. Given love, the unloved can become loving."

Know Your Own Responses to Trauma

When you know your own responses to trauma, you can model good responses for your family. Adult survivors of childhood trauma need to know what trauma meant for them and how it affected their psyche, sense of self, confidence, ability to trust and relate to others, intra- and inter-personal connectedness, and vulnerability to self-destructive habits like drug use, self-harm, and repeating the trauma cycle. It is important to listen to our inner voice and start to take better care of our needs; that helps us become more available for the people we love.

When I lose loved ones to a war zone, or hear bad news about family overseas, or when I have a difficult day at work, I try to look within and proceed with caution and compassion, so I can be fair to my needs and can also be available for my wife and children. It is a balance caregivers need to juggle daily.

Three things are important for a traumatized family: to find a coherent meaning in their experience through creating a new narrative, to make amends and have some form of self-forgiveness and closure, and to not repeat the cycle. Many patients come through the broken revolving doors of the healthcare system unable to get unstuck because they lost their voice to their trauma story, or because they believe in a distorted narrative that was imposed on them. The same is true for the families of caregivers. Do not let your silence or anyone else speak for you. Reclaim the podium and tell your own story.

Relational wounds heal relationally. Trauma survivors need to first regain some sense of safety and trust before they can share their narrative in a coherent way and before they can move toward finding meaning, exploring forgiveness, and having closure. Dr. Alisha Moreland-Capuia said that "The three ingredients for healing relational wounds are safety, truth, and reconciliation, and in that order."

Persistence and consistency pay, especially when combined with love and tender care. It is important for our loved ones, especially children, to have some sense of predictability. Children do not do well in chaos. The more we can have a routine that is flexible and takes into consideration all family members' needs, especially during times of uncertainty, the better the outcome for the whole family.

Choose one habit to develop at a time. Go from easiest to more challenging. What if you talk nicer to yourself twice as often as you do now? What if you eat more fruits or drink more water? What if you stop yourself from reacting impulsively twice as often as you do now? Take small but steady steps and celebrate small victories. When it comes to strengthening family ties, no victory is too small to celebrate.

Reaching out might be difficult when we feel down. That is why it is important to be part of a community of care that has members willing to reach in to check on each other. To accept support is not easy, but who said change was easy? Many times, change is scary and uncomfortable, yet it is often necessary. I was quite shy and introverted up until the war in Libya in 2011, and then I found myself in a position to advocate for and speak up on behalf of millions who were traumatized. I worked on mastering the art of keeping respectful eye contact, listening actively, engaging in deep dialogues, and extending a hand of kindness toward strangers. I did the same to bond with my children. That could be awkward at first, but it got easier with practice. When it comes to mending broken hearts, it is okay to "fake it until you make it." What a beautiful legacy we would leave for our children and in them if we helped co-create a world that is full of compassion and deep kindness.

Deep kindness is a principle that I borrow from Houston Kraft (2020), who wrote his book *Deep Kindness* to challenge all of us to move away from superficially pleasant relationships and into meaningful connections where we pay attention and show up for people, including those we do not know.

Engage in acts of love toward yourself. That will begin to fill your basic needs and emotional buckets. When you are a healthy parent, you can parent in healthy ways.

Trauma That Affects Children Needs to Be Tactfully Addressed

If trauma has already happened, parents and caregivers can intervene to create favorable outcomes for their children and families. Good intentions alone are not enough, though. Parents deserve to be equipped with the necessary tools to help them break the cycles of dysfunction caused by trauma. Trauma sometimes happens inside the house, but many times outside of it, including in schools, places of leisure, houses of worship, and in social gatherings. Busy caregivers might have the added burden of constantly worrying about the safety of their families. What really matters is that you are being an emotionally safe and available parent.

I recently conducted a survey to examine how strong the bond is between daughters and their fathers. The results showed that parents rated themselves as safe, caring, open, and available, but some were described by their children as the complete opposite. That disconnect does not mean that they are bad parents; no parent is. We all love our children, but many times we do not know how to show love.

That is why we created the Daughter-Father Bonding channel on YouTube and recorded over 60 videos to provide hands-on activities and practical tips for family bonding and healing, starting with establishing a solid foundation of safety and trust.

Children cope with stress in different ways. According to the Center for Adolescent Studies:

> Some of the biggest challenges children face during times of crisis are self-isolation; excessive screen time; conflicts caused by the strain of close quarters; separation from friends; and mourning milestone rituals. Sheltering-in-place caused by the COVID-19 pandemic for example tended to amplify existing personal and interpersonal problems because there is no escape valve from the people or the situation, no respite.

Some families, however, used that time to strengthen their connections. Merely surviving trauma is an act of courage, yet it would be wonderful if all of us, parents, make the conscious effort to bond with our loved ones early on, so we can tackle the aftermath of trauma together.

Trauma removes a child's sense of safety. Trauma makes it difficult for children to behave like kids. Family can help a traumatized child regain the belief in a safe world. Safe children trust in their worth and capabilities. The sense of safety comes from healthy attachment and the establishment of boundaries and structure, in addition to opportunities to play and have fun.

Children of trauma often use play as a way of speaking when they do not have the words to explain what happened to them. In a way, play becomes their voice. Parents need to watch closely for unhealthy coping and to show delight in the child at times of joy and distress. When children feel their parents' delight in them, they learn that getting exposed to trauma did not permanently damage them.

Help your children live their childhood

Children need to trust that their needs will be met consistently. That means we need to ensure they receive their due rights as much as we ask them to fulfill their responsibilities. It is not easy to give what you have not received, and it is exhausting to keep running on an empty tank. It is exhausting for your child and for you.

We need to allow activities as much as possible, be consistent and offer a warm style of parenting that is always available. Here are examples of activities toward that goal:

- establishing trust through dialogue—attentively listening to children's concerns and honestly trying to alleviate them
- spending extra time with the child, like a few extra minutes before bedtime
- going back to routines as soon as safely possible after the trauma
- accommodating every question and reaction
- correcting "negative" behaviors through nonviolent means
- self-monitoring and self-discipline for adults, too, because violence makes children doubt their worth
- pointing the child to healthy coping mechanisms in themselves and the environment
- assigning quality time to do family bonding activities

Spending quality time together can be done as a family exercise, like assigning 30 minutes of uninterrupted, technology-free, eye-to-eye, heart-to-heart time getting to enjoy your family, or taking the children on individual outings. Your children, and most likely you too, will enjoy that one-on-one undivided attention.

Let your loved ones know that they are okay the way they are. We need to let our children know that they are not broken, that we do not "fix" people. No one wants us to fight their fight or walk their walk. What is needed is a caring soul, a listening ear, a hand they can hold, and a shoulder they can lean on or cry on along the way.

Be there for your children

No one can give the child affection and a sense of safety more than the child's own parents. When the parent is physically or emotionally absent, it leaves a deep void in the child's heart that no one else can fill, and a wound in their psyche no one else can heal.

Why do some parents distance themselves from their children? What would cause a parent to shy away from attaching to their child, especially after trauma? Here are some possible answers:

- They had not established an open-door policy and comfort with their children back when things were "normal." I often see this with teenagers. They want to talk to us, but we do not know how to talk to them, and they are left to nurse their own wounds. Many cry themselves to sleep unnoticed. This is unfair to your children today and can haunt you as a parent tomorrow. When you come later wanting to talk to your teenage child, they might tell you that you have arrived too late. Scary, is it not?
- They are afraid they will cause more damage if they do not do it "right." The problem is that our children grow up very quickly and delaying bonding with them risks never bonding with them.
- They may not have attached as children, and the idea is foreign to them. But when it comes to our children's emotional

wellness, no water is too dangerous; it is okay to explore uncharted territories.

- They are so focused on other things that they do not notice their child is not attaching.

When a child is threatened by parental absence, they might
- take the role of the parent and carry excessive responsibilities on their shoulders, or hold themselves to unreasonable standards, which might lead to hostility or aggression in order to protect themselves and others;
- become anxious, which could manifest as irritability or hyperactivity;
- become fearful and either withdraw or isolate; or
- become depressed or suicidal.

Be encouraged to know that attachment can happen even later in life, especially when a person is helped to make meaningful sense of their trauma story. It is never too late to improve the bond with your family. When it comes to our loved ones, loving them is always the right thing to do. If your relationship with your loved ones needs healing, start now. You are a healer, so do not delay healing while it is still possible. I believe that healing our families is always possible. Better late than never.

Help children's developing identities

Model self-care, self-awareness, sharing, and listening. Trauma can impact core beliefs and shake the children's foundation of self-esteem and healthy identity. As parents, we need to be on the look-out for any self-loathing language or self-destructive behaviors that our children engage in, and we need to fill their emotional tanks and let them know that they are loved and valued, unconditionally. Parents have the keys to improving their children's self-worth, their world views, and eventually their psychosocial health and holistic well-being.

The story of Ted comes to mind here. His teacher told the class that she loved all of them the same, but in reality she had never liked Ted. He was always withdrawn and disheveled in addition to academically struggling. But when she found out that he had been the best student in the school until his mother died a year earlier, she took a special interest in him and he started to blossom. She believed in the child and he in turn came to believe in himself. If you believe in your child, anything becomes possible for them. Never clip your children's wings. Rather, help them achieve their full potential. We were all born unshackled.

To cope with difficult emotions, children might turn to risky behaviors, like violence, using alcohol or illicit drugs, excessive screen time, dangerous websites, or extremist ideology. Hurt people hurt people. Unfortunately, many children get traumatized, and because they do not share their trauma with their parents or do not find the words to describe what happened, they might show changes in language or behavior, such as lashing out or shutting down, and some will go to extremes and hurt themselves or others. Violence can be a manifestation of trauma, though bear in mind that not everyone who gets traumatized becomes violent, and not everyone who engages in violence has a history of trauma. Children should always speak up and reach out for help from grown-ups, hopefully their parents. Many children, for different reasons, do not speak up. As parents, therefore, we need to keep an eye on our children and intervene when we feel that something is not right. We build trust with our children by giving them reasonable freedom and independence, but we are always the ones behind the steering wheel. The world is a dangerous place, so let us be a coat of armor for our precious little ones.

Children sometimes confide in one another. That is wonderful, but they need to know their limits and when to speak up when things are overwhelming or unsafe. Supporting their friends by consulting with them and keeping their secrets can put too much pressure on these small shoulders. We need to teach our children through example that part of caring for others is caring for ourselves. This can look like the following: You tune in to their emotions and notice subtle changes. If they open their heart about a friend's struggle, you do not panic. Rather show them that big feelings are to be broken into small pieces to get digested.

Know your child's window of tolerance for stress

Anxiety can cause some children to regress into immature behaviors. There is a wide variation among individuals' "window of tolerance" for toxic stress and uncertainty. We need to know our own window of tolerance, too. If we are not aware of our limits, we might show irritability around our patients or peers, risking professional damage, or around the people we love, risking interpersonal damage.

When a child becomes emotionally distressed, they need to be listened to with full attention, their feelings acknowledged, their experience validated, and their options expanded. Rather than punishing a child who is acting out or denying their feelings, we need to show compassion and empathy, bear witness to the suffering, and look for the real underlying cause of their unwanted "bad" behavior. Parents can use the well-known STOP method to discourage an unwanted behavior (State the behavior you are observing and your feelings about it, Talk about preferred alternatives, Offer choices, and Provide reasonable consequences).

Unprocessed trauma can leave children emotionally stuck. And because trauma activates the limbic system (the emotional midbrain) and shuts down the cortex (the logical forebrain), children might struggle with mastering critical thinking skills and get caught up in daydreaming about, and reliving, their trauma, risking labels like ADHD or names like oppositional, defiant, learning disabled, and so on. That is why I am an advocate for social emotional learning and psychosocial education rather than focusing only on catching up academically. This is true in the aftermath of a pandemic, but really after any trauma.

BE THEIR ANCHOR

If you do not talk to your child, someone else will.

If you do not listen to your child, someone else will.

If you do not notice your child, someone else will.

If you do not sit with your child, someone else will.

If you do not befriend your child, someone else will.

Be that someone your child is looking for.

Model unconditional love

How do we challenge and counteract our children's distorted thinking patterns that are telling them no one loves them and that there is no hope for them? We do that by showing them that we love and believe in them unconditionally. We do it with our words and our actions. Our children hear us say:

- "I value my children above everything else."
- "I love coming home to be with my family."
- "I believe the sky is the limit for my kids."

They watch us set aside other things to be with them. They see us rearrange space in our busy schedules to spend time with them. They feel us when we hold them and when we sit, laugh, talk, and play together. These kinds of words and actions gradually disprove the beliefs they hold that they are not worthy, and open the doors to self-acceptance, self-love, and eventually self-healing.

Our children might resort to unhealthy habits to cope with self-doubt. One example of that is unhealthy eating habits. Reassure them in their concerns about body image. Many children, boys and girls, might hide their suffering from their parents because of stigma or because they do not want to be "a burden." They might go to extremes of unhealthy dieting or vigorous exercising to try to fit the stereotype that the media displays as "the perfect body." It is important for parents to love their children and let them know that their bodies are perfect the way they are, that they are beautiful inside and out, and that they are unconditionally loved and accepted.

Defuse the invincibility defense mechanism. According to the Center for Adolescent Studies, children's need for individuation and self-determination can complicate adhering to safety protocols like those imposed during the COVID pandemic. There is an "invincibility defense mechanism" that allows them to take risks, but since their brains are still developing, it is harder for them to process the fact that their behavior during crises matters. They hold tight to subconsciously perceived rites of passage. That is why during the pandemic we would see teens gather in large groups and ignore instructions about masking and social distancing. That is a behavior that needs understanding, not criminalizing.

Part of tending to your soul is tending to your family and looking after loved ones. Family is the foundation of healthy individuals and the glue that holds loved ones together in times of both distress and delight. When the world becomes dangerous or unpredictable, family is a healing environment and a safe space. Family should be an umbrella of unconditional love and acceptance where everyone feels safe and at ease to be their true self. A home is supposed to be a refuge, not a prison cell. It is a place where we blossom, not wither away. Many of our coping styles, defense mechanisms, and traumatic adaptations stem from our family dynamics. Many parents want their children to be "perfect," but connection, not perfection, is what matters. The energy we spend on perfection takes away from the joy and quality of the connection. When it comes to our children, we think the best of them and give our best to them. What we say sticks; they take on what we are, so who we are matters.

Talking about trauma as a family takes away some of its power over us. Not everything we inherit is worth passing on to our children, especially not a distorted trauma story. Let us invite our family to write a new narrative, one that moves us toward meaning, healing, and closure. As a family, we should treat our loved ones with the highest level of grace. That might mean caregivers learning new skills and applying unfamiliar tools. Being invested parents might even mean we become children again. Jump in and join them, try it, it is loads of fun.

WHAT HELPS WITH HEALING?

- Safe and nurturing relationships between parents, children, and the extended family will help you recover and grow after trauma.
- Fun can bring healing, so have some fun. It is said that laughter is the best medicine, and that families that play together stay together. Families living with trauma need the medicine of enjoying each other. Love is a medicine that you can never overdose on; the more the better.

- Families that engage in bonding activities will have an easier time opening channels of communication, building bridges of trust, and creating long-lasting memories.

When to Seek Professional Assistance

A specialist might be needed when a child has prolonged symptoms of anxiety, sorrow, anger, or grief; if their academic or social performance is declining; if they are suffering from recurrent nightmares or night terrors; if they are hallucinating or having paranoid or obsessive symptoms; if they isolate; if they start to use alcohol or other drugs, if they have severe psychosomatic manifestations like migraines or startle (non-epileptic) seizures; if they regress in age with behaviors such as bed-wetting, thumb-sucking, stuttering, or clinging to their caregiver; if they neglect their basic needs, engage in deviant ideologies or activities; and/or if they are suicidal or homicidal or have access to weapons and lethal means.

When one member of the family struggles, the whole family suffers. There is no shame in reaching out for help. There are many resources available for you to heal your family. As with body organs, when a family member heals from an injury, the whole body moves toward healing and a state of equilibrium.

Keep a Healthy Work-Family Balance

Caregivers might fulfill their children's materialistic needs, but due to long working hours and many other competing commitments, they might neglect the children's emotional needs. Many of our children end up going to bed with a full stomach and an empty heart. Some cry themselves to sleep, some find comfort in going online to share deep feelings with total strangers who might be predators, while others use drugs or even engage in self-harm to fill that emotional void. I call that "losing the American dream chasing it." Our families are the dream. Our children not only crave our attention, they deserve it.

I am reminded here of the story of a young boy who kept asking his father, "How much do you make an hour?" Finally the irritated father asked why this question, and the boy said, "I've been saving money to buy one hour of your time that we can spend together."

Here are some things we need to keep in mind:

- Our job is not only to protect our families but also to heal them.
- Trauma loses its power to ruin us when we face it with love and hope.
- We are the ones who can help our family heal, through our unconditional love.
- We cannot meaningfully care for others without taking care of ourselves too.
- We need to open channels of communication and build bridges of trust with our loved ones.
- Our love supports the physical, emotional, and spiritual well-being of our children.
- We need to build support systems. It takes a village to heal a child.
- Trauma usually comes from the threat to safety or the loss of control over our circumstances.
- Parents might need to learn new tools to help their families navigate the healing journey.
- Children need attention and caring love to meet their breathtaking full potential.

- Children need to believe that the world is a safe place and that adults can be trusted.
- If the world is not a safe or kind place, at least let us make our homes places of kindness and safety, always.
- When children feel safe, they start to act safely.
- Emotional needs, not only materialistic ones, are important.
- The most fortunate parent is the one whose children feel safe around them.
- Safety and trust can come from simple acts of love, like keeping eye contact, smiling, greeting, safe touch, listening attentively, talking respectfully, and spending quality time together.
- The good news is that attachment and healing can happen, even if late. Hold on to hope.
- It is important to have a flexible structure, with rules, chores, rewards, and consequences.
- Love is unconditional. Each child is unique. Love them uniquely.
- Expressing emotions is a sign of strength, and vulnerability is the ultimate act of courage.
- We must each consider what legacy we would like to leave for, and in, our children.
- In our relationship with our loved ones, connection, and not perfection, is the goal.
- What we say sticks. Let us say things that build them up and fill them with hope and self-love.

Love and hope can help heal the invisible wounds of trauma and untangle the deadly web of family dysfunction. Trauma loses its destructive power when love and hope step in.
- Trauma terrifies; love and hope comfort.

- Trauma destroys; love and hope build.
- Trauma separates; love and hope unite.
- Trauma breaks hearts; love and hope mend them.

Caregivers might come home exhausted or totally depleted, not having the mental capacity to be around their loved ones in meaningfully empowering ways. They might have nothing left in themselves to give. The problem is that there is no one else who can do this job, not a babysitter and not another adult. As a parent, you have no substitute; you are irreplaceable. That is why it is vital that you pay attention to your needs so you can help fulfill the needs of your family. When you are showing safe and healthy boundaries, you SOOTHE your loved ones:

- Safety and hope are equally important foundations of a healthy home.
- Offer plenty of options.
- Organize their experience through flexible and joyful structure that they help co-create.
- Talk about any family issues collaboratively. This might mean skillfully talking about your own trauma.
- Help them find solutions, services, and resources, so they do not always rely only on you.
- Empower them and expand their horizons.

Resource 2.1: House of Joy

Here are a few thoughts on how to bring healing to your family dynamics, through bonding and the power of LOVE (Listening, Options, Validation, and Empowerment).

SAFETY: We all need to feel safe at home in order to meet our full potential and contribute to our society in a productive and meaningful way. Violence in any of its forms should have no place in our homes. A house full of violence will not feel like home. Violence can lead to serious social and psychological impacts, shattering self-worth and the sense of trust in a safe world. Children deserve to feel safe around their parents and caregivers. They should not feel they have to walk on eggshells at home. The most unfortunate parent is the one who makes their family feel unsafe when they enter the house and whose children breathe easier after they exit, and the luckiest parent is the one who prioritizes loving their loved ones.

UNCONDITIONAL LOVE: Love that is not based on something our loved ones do, but rather has no conditions. Yes, it is wonderful when they do good, work hard, and try their best, but we have joy and delight in the relationship regardless.

THE POWER OF SMILING: When we smile, our bodies produce good hormones, and when we frown, they release bad chemicals. Smiling is an act of charity. Unfortunately, when you smile at people, they might think you did something wrong, judge you as being "weird," or think you need something from them. That is, if they even notice. Many people these days are so busy with their phones and other gadgets that they barely make a human connection. But we should not give up on something good because it is not popular. Smiling never goes out of style. A smile is a gift we should offer to everyone we meet, especially our families. Charity starts at home.

EYE CONTACT: If we do not pay attention to our children, it might be too late to notice the issues that bother them. We need to bond with them today because tomorrow might be too late. Invest in your children right now. Notice the small issues before they get complicated. When your children come to you, get off your phone, turn off your computer, log off your "social" media, drop everything else, and look them in the eye. That will make them feel safe in the relationship they have with you. Love starts with us paying attention to the people we love.

GREETING: A warm greeting affirms to the people we meet that they are safe with us. It assures the other person that I mean peace, not harm, and that I am a safe person. When someone insults you or wants to engage you in useless or hateful speech, safely disengage and simply walk away. We spread a greeting of peace to everyone regardless of their background, and who is more deserving than our loved ones?

SAFE TOUCH: Safe touch is an important tool for bonding with our children, especially after trauma. Many children, unfortunately, do not feel safe or comfortable giving their parents hugs or holding hands with them; do not settle for that. If there is a dysfunction in your household, do not accept it as the norm. There is nothing normal about family breakdown. Revolt against the unhealthy status quo. You can change the narrative and the trajectory for your family even if you came to this late. Better late than never.

LISTENING AND TALKING: Listening is an active form of love. There is a whole art to how to talk so children listen and how to listen when children talk. Many children reply to their parents' questions with "Fine" and "Nothing," and some parents may feel frustrated with that style of communication and even start to think that their children are being disrespectful. But in fact, most children do not mean harm when they speak that way. Sometimes it is the way these questions are asked or the timing. I mean, no one likes to answer too many questions at once, particularly when they first come home, especially if the questioning feels like an interrogation. Children can express themselves respectfully and let their parents know that they will be ready to talk later, and parents should appreciate that we all need some space to unwind, especially after a long day at work or school. Home is a place where we can catch our breath and unwind. Home should not be where we feel suffocated.

As parents, we can make or break our children:
- build them up or tear them down
- empower or discourage them
- reassure or shut them off
- inspire or depress them
- welcome or reject them

QUALITY TIME: In a family context, it is sad when someone is missing physically, but it is heartbreaking when they are missing emotionally. Many parents spend long hours away from their children because they are working to provide for the family. A family is a group of people connected by birth or marriage. They have different personalities, but stick together through whatever comes their way, the good and the bad. That is a wonderful definition of a family, yet many families do not feel that way. In fact, sometimes family members behave like enemies, especially after trauma. Trauma can make or break a family. That is why it is important to spend quality family time together. There are many ways a family can establish a routine of having family time. This is of course flexible, and each family is unique, but I recommend a block of time every day of technology-free time spent together. Sit together, look each other in the eye, and open your hearts to talk about things that are important for you as a family.

It is also important for families to know how to interact during a conflict. In our home, we do not allow foul language, we call out passive aggression, and we use our words, not our hands, to resolve arguments and prevent fights. We express our emotions, manage our anger, and never hurt each other. We tackle issues as a team. That is what family is about. We stick together through thick and thin.

When Arjun appealed to Joy's parents, despite their anger they called in and said their final goodbyes. Joshua even flew in to be with his sister, who died holding his hand, with a big smile on her face.

One thing we can do for our children is teach them responsibility. Many parents try to protect children from difficult emotions and big feelings. They sometimes go to extremes to shelter them from discomfort. However, we should prepare our children for the real world, a world where they have tasks and responsibilities assigned to them, and where they make choices and face the consequences of their decisions. A child should be assigned age-appropriate chores to appreciate being part of the household and to feel like a valued member of the family. You can even do chores as a bonding exercise. Some families turn tasks into fun activities and use that time to get closer.

Talking about respect is also a common theme in the family context. We are humans, and all of us make mistakes, and that is okay as long as we try to improve. When we do something wrong as parents, we can allow our children to respectfully tell us about it and appreciate them for that. Respect is shown through actions, not only words, and it is a two-way street. When children receive respect, they reciprocate, and that makes the relationship much more enjoyable.

We also need to take advantage of being young, strong, and healthy, and also benefit from free time and not waste it. What are some ways we can use time in a productive way? We can read or listen to something useful. To watch or read or hear something that makes us gain useful knowledge is to spend time well. There are of course different ways to spend our time, like learning a new skill or helping others. We can spend time together as a family, but also allow people some free personal time. We all need our private space and breathing room. Time together should never be a source of stress. If parenting feels like a burden or comes across as a daunting task, then it is not being done right.

A family also has rules. Something that is commonly misunderstood is how parents can discipline their children. Adults should never insult or hurt children. We need to be role models. We should never hurt anyone with our actions or our words. Rather, we invest time and energy in our children and tend to their emotional and psychosocial needs. Our children deserve to have their best affirmed and their worst redirected.

Resource 2.2: This Is Us, Together

The truth is that trauma has impacted your family. There is no getting around it, but there are ways through it. You and your family may have more to untangle than families not terrorized by trauma, and you may feel at times like healing is impossible or out of reach.

Sometimes simply saying what has happened and acknowledging it together can get the healing process started, even though other therapeutic interventions may be necessary.

Here are things that might be true for your family right now:

- We have been traumatized.
- My children and I do not talk much.
- I do not know what to do.
- I feel guilty.
- I want to be a good parent, but I do not know how.
- I find myself making things worse.
- I am an overprotective parent.
- I am preoccupied with the trauma that has happened.
- I prefer to focus on visible wounds, not invisible ones.
- I chase after solutions to my physical needs more than my emotional ones.
- In our home, the F-word we avoid is *Feelings*.
- I notice people walking on eggshells around me.
- I feel hopeless and afraid most of the time.
- My children seem to feel bad about themselves.
- I feel uncomfortable around my loved ones.
- I tend to either isolate or lash out, and the easy target for my outbursts is my family.

If these dynamics are true in your home, I have some good news for you. There is hope.

One of the most helpful steps to healing can begin right now, with you.

I call it your "This Is Us, Together" Declaration. Together, you can declare what is true now, and together you can declare what you want your future to be.

Remember Joy? Her drug use caused all kinds of family chaos. But when Arjun reached out to her parents and to her brother Josh, he used parts of this declaration to remind them of the love they always had for their daughter.

Here is an example of a "This Is Us, Together" Declaration:
- We are a family that stands together, like a team.
- We have experienced trauma.
- We are more resilient because of our trauma story.
- We will not let the past ruin our future.
- We were together through the trauma, and we will stay together through future struggles.
- We respect one another's right to heal in our own ways.
- We do not let each other struggle alone.
- We will not hide our pain to protect one another.
- We will do whatever we need to do to bring healing.
- We will be there for each other because we are worth it.
- We are strong, smart, brave, kind, and determined.
- We listen to and learn from one another.
- We use our trauma as a proof of our strength, and not as an excuse for negative behaviors.
- We make our home a safe, kind, and caring place.
- We are each other's shields and have zero tolerance for any form of violence.
- We tackle issues as a team.

- We use every single resource available to us.
- We believe loving one another is our greatest healing power. How do families go about creating their "This Is Us, Together" Declaration?

Families are different in their degree of comfort about things like this. For a family that is securely attached, a family meeting could be the way to go. For families that are more distant, there are gentle approaches to being with your family without being intrusive or coming across as fake. It is the being-with and your physical and emotional availability that matter.

If you are a hands-on family, jump in and create your declaration. Otherwise, find a tender way to introduce the activity to your family, something that works for you and is comfortable for them. Do not overthink it, though. Be sincere and trust your intuition. Love is the best remedy, so try it, starting now.

When trauma strikes, practice lots of self-compassion. It is okay at times to not feel okay. Be graceful with yourself, and graceful with others. Times of distress need all of us to practice generous amounts of patience and self-love.

I would like to conclude this section with a plea to caregivers. If your relationship with your loved ones is struggling or dying, try the triple-A approach: pay attention to the "small" things happening in your home that usually go unnoticed, show appreciation for your family through your words and actions, and express affection by being emotionally safe and available. Do not delay this; start today. Your family is worth it. You are worth it.

Reflection Corner

Welcome to this sacred space. This is a breathing room. It is for you to pause and reflect in if you wish to do so.

Thank you for your commitment.

You have seen the impact of caregiving on your family.

Take your time to heal from the pain of your trauma so you can find the joy of interacting with your loved ones.

I invite you to do something kind to your mind, like:
- Think positively about yourself.
- Challenge negative and self-loathing language.
- Live the current moment, without regrets about the past or anxieties about the future.

3 / Addressing Systemic Trauma

Physicians, nurses, and other healthcare staff risk their lives to save the lives of their patients. They stay away from their families to ensure that everyone else stays safe with theirs. The least we can all do to honor the sacrifices of caregivers on the frontlines is to show respect, if not gratitude.

I am acutely aware that caregivers are not a homogeneous group. They come from diverse backgrounds and react and respond to issues in unique ways. There might be common themes, but not a single statement in this book is intended to be a generalization.

Because vulnerability is a sign of courage, I invite you to attune to your authentic self and appeal to your high moral values. The field of caregiving is full of beauty, but it has a dark side too. We can work on deep issues not by pointing fingers or assigning blame, but by brainstorming practical solutions and dismantling dysfunctional and outdated systems like those that condone racist and discriminatory policies and practices. Hate is a pandemic that we can, and we should, tackle together, preferably proactively rather than reactively, not only to make the world a better place for us, but also for the sake of our children and future generations.

I cannot afford to not speak up. I have seen the deadly impact of hate, and it is my mission and moral obligation to combat injustice, in all its forms.

My hope and intention is to open safe spaces and honest conversations around these too-often ignored topics. The goal is not for you to feel guilty or defeated, but rather for you to get empowered or hopefully even inspired. I know that I cannot do justice to the topic of institutional trauma or cover it in detail, and I am also aware that we cannot talk about hate without talking about historical trauma and the legacy of oppression, about racism-infested systems and institutions, and about privilege and current-day politics. I am inviting you here to take a small first step toward healing these phenomena because I refuse to remain a silent bystander or give false testimony. I owe it to my children, and you owe it to yours, to speak up for justice. Our children deserve better.

Caregiver Trauma and Healing Within the Healthcare Industry: Cultures and Supports

Caregivers are to be valued and treasured; hopefully they too can view themselves as valuable treasures. Charles Figley (1995) urges us to treasure and tend to those who treat the traumatized. But how can you treasure yourself? You do that when you believe in how valuable you are to the system you work in, to those you serve, to your loved ones, and mainly to yourself.

Healers are focused on healing. When they come to their places of healing, they usually assume that "the system" will protect and support them, but sometimes they find out the hard way that this is not the case. Here is a story to illustrate how caregivers need to be vocal and actively engaged in changing dysfunctional systems that can both literally and figuratively suffocate them.

She Can't Breathe

"Code gray, emergency room, code gray, all available staff and security to the ED, room number four, STAT," announced the now-panicking hospital operator over the intercom.

Along with many of his ED colleagues, Alex, a 58-year-old Latino registered nurse, rushed to the room to find the patient choking Tiffany, one of the ED nurses, who was fighting for her life, unable to breathe, and about to pass out.

"Take him down, take him down!" "Let go of her, now!" "Protect her airways!" Multiple staff members were shouting as they struggled to bring down the highly agitated patient. It took most of them and a number of injuries to take him to the ground before security finally arrived to place him in restraints, while a few rushed to the aid of the nurse, who was quite shaken and struggling to catch her breath. They took turns making sure she was okay.

"Tiff, honey, are you alright?"

"Let's make sure you're physically okay."

"Cervical collar, then to MRI, STAT."

"Tiff, darling, I'll drive you home as soon as you're ready."

"Do you want me to call anyone?"

"Hey, you guys, I'll be okay, I promise! You're all amazing, you saved my life, you're so sweet. I'm alright, seriously, I'm just in shock. I didn't see that one coming; I did nothing to set him off."

"Tiffany, you're taking the day off tomorrow, nonnegotiable," announced the charge nurse, fighting back tears.

"Keep us posted, Tiff."

"Text me when you get home."

Staff made sure their colleague got home safely, then huddled to debrief.

"We deserve to feel safe. We didn't sign up to be threatened or assaulted," Alex announced, discouraged and outraged.

"You're absolutely right, Alex," added Laila, another nurse. "Administration thinks getting attacked is an occupational hazard. They claim toxic stress is something that comes with the territory, and getting traumatized is to be expected. I guess they want us to just suck it up."

"Well, they're wrong," replied Alex. "This is a cycle that needs to be broken, and that happens only when all of us speak up, when we raise our voices and make a big noise. I'm tired of this. Every day it's the same thing here: We take care of people, and some of them wouldn't hesitate to hurt us. I'm tired. My safety and sanity, my physical and mental health, and that of my family, are too precious, too valuable for me to risk getting traumatized every time I set foot in this place."

"I agree, Alex," Laila said in despair. "People romanticize working in the emergency room. They don't know the heavy price we pay every day for being caregivers and the fires we're constantly walking through and extinguishing. It's such a difficult profession; I feel like a soldier on the front line of a war that never ends, and I don't know what to do about it. Nothing seems to ever change."

"But I know what I'm going to do," said Alex, determined. "I'm demanding an immediate meeting with the ED leadership. There need to be major changes to ensure our safety. We've the right to know every patient's risk of violence, and suicide, too, before they get assigned to us. What's next? Someone bringing a gun and opening fire?"

"Go get 'em, Alex!" "Thank you for speaking up for the team!" His teammates took turns showing him support and gratitude.

The above scenario is not that uncommon. Assaults on staff happen too often to be ignored. When a staff member is injured, the system scrambles to respond. Caregivers like Alex need to know that it is never okay to expect to get hurt on the job. Many caregivers remain silent when they get assaulted, they brush that incident off as it was "no big of a deal." They need to speak up, however, and demand modifications that help guarantee their safety. To get hurt is a big deal. Safety is one of our very basic needs.

Another very serious phenomenon in our field that we seldom talk about is the insulting and humiliating ways our female colleagues are treated. Medicine is infested with sexism and sexual violence; it makes me sick. A caregiver on the frontline who is leaving behind her family, sacrificing her comfort, and risking her safety does not deserve to be subjected to any kind of abusive language or behavior. I want her to feel safe to speak up, and I will always be an ally in her fight against sexual trauma, especially one that happens within the walls of our "healing" systems.

Sometimes Leaving Is Better Than Half Staying

If your place of work is toxic, then find an environment that matches your gifts. It is important, writes Dr. Jack Krasuski, to work with a system that aligns with your ideals and that values you, serving patients' best interests but also tackling issues that affect your flourishing. You, too, deserve to be provided safety—physical, sexual, psychological, social, financial, and spiritual. I have worked with systems that reacted very differently to my passion about global health and my desire to serve in my local community and in refugee camps. One system asked that I "make a choice" between my job and my calling. Well, that was an easy choice to make; I walked away.

You do not need to work in a toxic environment. There is always a better job waiting to welcome you. Remember that your current behavior is getting you what you are getting, so if what you are getting is not what you want, then change your behavior. To do the same thing over and over again expecting a different result is the very definition of insanity. You cannot keep insisting that you are safe while you are clearly sinking in quicksand. If there is a mismatch between you and your environment, either mold yourself to fit in or mold the environment to fit your needs. If you cannot find a culture that matches what you want, build one.

One of my colleagues runs a "virtual sanctuary" to help staff establish a community of care where they can process their collective trauma in a safe and empowering space. If such a space does not exist where you work, look beyond the constraints of your locale or start your own support circle.

Tend to Your Soul

The field of caregiving can revive, or crush, our souls. Caregivers absorb traumatic stories of others, and that weighs heavily on our emotions. Before we can treat or prevent, we need to understand what happens to our body, psyche, heart, and soul when we absorb the traumatic stories of others. The *Encyclopedia of Trauma* (Figley, 2012) talks about the repeated blows that do not immediately knock us out: "These are the ones we overlook but are likely the most dangerous."

Long-term involvement and investment in emotionally demanding situations takes its toll on the soul. We have a duty to warn our students and junior colleagues about the "occupational hazard" of our work. We should not accept it as "collateral damage" or something that "comes with the territory." No one signs up to get burned-out. In taking care of ourselves, there should be no conflict between our professional needs and our personal ones. On the contrary. The more we thrive personally, the more we blossom professionally.

Work stress is *not* a requirement for success. According to Dr. Bryan Robinson:

> many professionals believe the myth that work stress is a prerequisite to get ahead in their careers. But science shows the opposite is true, that work stress truncates our career trajectory. If we are in the habit of sacrificing our well-being to meet work demands, we cannot be the best version of ourselves. Self-care prepares us to give more to our jobs. When we put ourselves first, there is more of us to go around.

Robinson adds that "Top-notch companies that make employees' self-care a priority, boost their bottom line."

Know and contribute to your community of care. Find or build one that fits you. Each group of caregivers creates a unique culture. Some teams externalize their feelings and normalize emotional expression, while others internalize feelings and shame them. That is why a community of care can supplement solitary acts of self-care, which, for the most part, get neglected. A community of care holds its members accountable for loving themselves and reminding each of them that they all count. Imagine being part of a team that genuinely cares about your holistic wellness and does so through engaging all its members in deep kindness rather than just the superficial pleasantries we exchange and the empty words we offer one another.

Caring Systems

Your institutional culture can reinforce or mitigate stress. According to *Compassion Fatigue* by Charles Figley (1995), here are some institutional measures and attitudes that might help mitigate compassion fatigue:

- The stressors are accepted as real and legitimate.
- The problems are viewed as institutional rather than being attributed to the individual caregiver.
- The approach is focused on solutions rather than on assigning blame.
- Support is expressed clearly, directly, and abundantly.
- The communication is open and effective.
- There is a high degree of cohesion and considerable flexibility of roles.
- Resources are utilized efficiently.
- There is no cultural tolerance of any form of violence, aggression, oppression, or retaliation.

Support programs can provide stress mitigation in response to stress. According to Jeffrey Mitchell, of the Critical Incident Stress Management (CISM) network, effective support programs need to be

- comprehensive;
- integrative;
- systematic;
- fully supportive, not merely offering therapy;
- multitactical;
- linked to resources; and
- run by peers.

Systems of care can be a source of pain and distress for employees. But when caregivers invest in self-care and healing, when they get comfortable asserting their boundaries and speaking up for their rights, and when they use proactive measures to take care of their needs, these systems can become a source of joy and delight.

Dismantle Traumatizing Systems; Build Cultures That Care

Systems we work with can be quite toxic, crushing our souls and limiting our potential to show up as our best authentic selves. Broken systems are in urgent need of rehabilitation, if not dismantling. Here are a few suggestions for caregivers to try to bring change to dysfunctional work environments.

Make sure that you use your community of support at times of stress. Interpersonal networks are powerful in promoting recovery. Part of holistic healing is making sure that you have social support networks you can rely on.

Recognize that healing involves the body, mind, heart, and soul. Many people, including some caregivers, trivialize, criticize, and discourage the use of psychosocial interventions. They base their disapproval on the argument that resources are to be allocated to the "most urgent needs." Visible wounds would win the argument over invisible ones any day.

I see that when I visit war zones and refugee camps, but I also see it whenever an organization deals with a sentinel event or other significant trauma: The focus goes to the perceived immediate survival needs, while the emotional impact gets "tabled" for a later time. The body of research and my own clinical experience show, however, that there are problems with such an approach. ACEs and other traumatic encounters have toxic impacts, with grave consequences for the long-term overall health and wellness of individuals, families, communities, and systems. Healing and wellness are holistic concepts, in which our invisible wounds need to be tended to and healed.

I have deep respect for the work of many international non-governmental organizations (NGOs). Some, however, have a very rigid approach to how they conduct business and use resources. I remember how one organization asked me what they could do with a $2,000 budget that they had to spend in Libya before the end of the day, or the amount would be taken away from future funding. I was very excited to point out that six neighborhoods in Benghazi could use playgrounds as avenues for play and art activities for children, and that each playground was expected to cost about $300. After staff contacted headquarters, the $2,000 budget could not be allocated to the playground project, and instead it went toward pizza and soda for the staff's goodbye party.

We all have the right to not only survive, but also thrive. Never take that right away from the people you serve or from your coworkers, no matter how they might make you feel. Remember that the person in front of you is someone's loved one. What you see might be viewed as a "difficult behavior," but, looked at from a trauma-informed lens, it might also be a traumatic adaptation. Look at the whole context. Trauma does not excuse traumatizing others, but it might explain the behavior you are observing, and that makes it easier for you to engage more empathically. Remember that the behavior is only the message; the person is trying to invite you to discover the deeper issue(s), the root cause(s). Accept that invitation safely or find someone to refer them to. We all lose our voice to trauma at times, and then we use behaviors to express our needs. Help people find their voice. It might take you only a short minute, but it has the potential to change someone's life, help transform lives. These concepts worked for me both professionally and personally. When my children "misbehave," I make the deliberate choice of spending a few extra minutes of heart-to-heart conversations with them. That helps me dig deeper to explore both the pain of what they are struggling with and the joy of being a parent entrusted with these tender souls.

Workplace Systems Can Contribute to Burnout

According to Jack Krasuski of the American Physician Institute, burnout is usually the result of a dysfunctional system, rather than something that is fundamentally wrong with the caregiver. There is an "unspoken contract" we assume exists that states that when I am working hard, "someone" is going to take care of me. Such contract is but an illusion. Krasuski adds that administration is not evil, rather taxed. Everyone is working to their maximum capacity. Unless you feel empowered, no one will anticipate your needs or frankly have the willpower to check on you. Everybody feels they are sinking. There are no saviors. You are the person you have been waiting for.

According to him, work-related causes of extreme burnout include

- paperwork (number one reason),
- unfriendly work environment,
- lack of autonomy,
- emotionally draining encounters with clients and their loved ones, and
- long working hours and heavy caseloads.

Krasuski urges, "Do not place yourself at the back of the line. Stop sinking in quicksand." We do not show up authentically as our best when we are burned out.

I remember taking a group of teenagers on a trauma-informed retreat. We were greeted warmly by the resort staff the first morning, but they were rather curt the next day. We found out that a large group of women had come before us to celebrate Mother's Day. Staff felt threatened and overwhelmed, and consequently they were running out of grace.

Caregivers, when supported, will find the joy, not only the pain, of caregiving, and they will continue to enthusiastically serve. Otherwise, we will be expecting them to act like robots and zombies with fake smiles and crushed spirits. This toxic cycle needs to be broken, for our sake, and also for the sake of our clients, our families, and the systems we operate within.

Suicide: The Ultimate Price of Burnout

In her deeply emotional book, *Physician Suicide Letters—Answered*, Dr. Pamela Wible (2016) takes us behind the fragile glamour of the white coat into a dark side of the healthcare profession that we seldom talk about—the deadly impact of toxic stress on the bodies, minds, hearts, and souls of healers. Her chilling dedication gives me goosebumps: "To all those who have lost their lives in pursuit of healing others." That resonated deeply with me, as the same words were chanted during the 2011 civil war in my home country, Libya: "We die so our country can live." I wonder why anyone must die for passionately caring about a cause.

Wible continues, "Even though I still have a sparkle in my eyes and joy in my heart, a piece of me is missing, I can never get it back." This is what caring does; it has a way of deeply touching our souls. She wonders if the rigidly analytical part of medicine is crushing our creative spirit. I commonly see that when the amount of paperwork takes away from the quality time I can spend with my clients. In a way, I talk more with the electronic charts than with the actual patients. She describes the medical profession as "A culture that condones hazing, bullying, sexual harassment, and teaching by public humiliation." She describes parts of her early journey in medical school: "As long as my tears kept flowing, I knew I would be okay. Crying meant I could still feel." She describes the pressures she felt: "After a decade of seven-minute visits at assembly-line clinics, I was nothing more than a factory worker." She refers to the tragic suicide of a doctor as the "Ultimate oxymoron, a healer who was unable to find healing. Suicide among caregivers is a symptom of the system, not a permanent condemnation of the caregiver. A suicidal caregiver is not defective; our profession is. When a caregiver takes their own life, it means that the field of medicine has lost its soul."

Per Dr. Wible (2016): "Standard treatment plan: for suicidal caregivers, suck it up, for caregiver's suicide, sweep it under the rug."

Caregiver suicide is an ugly phenomenon. It devastates the care team, and even the whole system. It is one of the best-kept secrets in our industry, and we can no longer remain silent. It is a shame if we do not speak up. Here is a story to illustrate that.

Heroes Are Not Supposed to Die

"Code blue, parking garage, lower level." A woman had jumped from the top of the hospital's parking structure and landed hard on the concrete floor. Staff gathered, responding to the frantic overhead announcement.

"Oh my God, staff, she's one of our docs," someone shouted.

Staff rushed their colleague to the emergency room, desperately trying to revive the still body.

"No, no, come on now, Darlene, please, don't you dare, please don't die," screamed one of the ED physicians performing CPR, desperately trying to resuscitate his coworker.

"Did someone call the family? Page the chaplain!" Staff scrambled to undo the crisis and erase the horror they had just witnessed.

In the ED reflection room, the chaplain and the hospital admin team met with the distraught parents, while staff from different units arrived in large numbers to relieve the ED staff. Everybody was restless. The emergency room seemed as if it had just been hit by explosives.

"Oh Mr. and Mrs. Hummingbird, I'm terribly sorry. She looked perfectly fine this morning. Oh my God, not my Darlene," cried Nina, a 35-year-old Native American addiction therapist, as she hugged the grieving parents, mourning the death of her best friend, an emergency room physician, by suicide.

Hysterically crying and almost going into a full-blown panic, Nina was conflicted, wanting to be honest about how she felt but also wanting to protect and not overwhelm the dear family.

Next day, the ED staff and those who had responded to

the code gathered to debrief. "I don't want to sound ungrateful," Nina announced, quite agitated, "But rather than offering tea for the soul and bringing us cookies and music, which I frankly find insulting, how come administration hasn't said a word about the suicide of one of our very own? Screw this, I responded to the code. I never imagined that one day I'd be performing CPR on Darlene." Nina shook her head in disbelief. "Oh my God, not Dr. Hummingbird, I still can't believe it. She looked extra beautiful and peaceful in the morning. No one saw it coming. She was smiling as she always does. She was going the extra mile to cheer everyone up. But I guess she didn't feel supported. I mean, I feel horrible. What could I have done differently? How could I have missed it? How come we couldn't prevent this?" Nina was now sobbing.

"This is terrible, Nina," replied Bailey, another addiction counselor. "I'm so very sorry for your loss—our loss, that is. Yes, Dr. Hummingbird was such a shining star, one of the sweetest souls you could ever meet. It's a shame that she couldn't find the support she needed in a system she helped build from scratch. We don't know what was going on in her personal life and we should respect her privacy, which is her family's request. My understanding is that she didn't have children; at least that's a good thing, I guess. But her poor parents—the most painful thing is to bury your own child. And dying by suicide has likely made it much harder."

"How can one of our colleagues, someone we see every day, find no solace being around us, and not trust any of us to confide in? How could a crowded place like our emergency room feel this lonely and desperate for Darlene?" said Helen, an emergency room nurse. "I'm not sure how we can ever recover after losing one of our teammates."

"Grief is a communal affair," interjected José, an ED social worker. "Maybe the best thing we can do to celebrate Darlene's memory is to build a community of care. Obviously, self-care done in isolation isn't enough. Maybe we can spend a few extra minutes to check on each other, to watch out, to pay attention and notice subtle changes, to make sure everyone is okay—really okay, that is—and make that a daily practice and part of the culture."

"I wish administration would listen," Nina said, now furious. "I've submitted a number of proposals before for staff wellness. I've always feared something like this would happen. I told admin how toxic the environment is down here, and the answer is always the same: they loved the idea, but they don't have the budget or resources to support it. They give us a Band-Aid, lip service, a few politically correct words to shut us up and make them feel better about themselves. It's so frustrating. It shouldn't have to take the death of a staff person for the system to wake up, the system that shames us for struggling through the toxic stress and the burnout it creates. The system that watches our every move and questions even our need for lunch and bathroom breaks will act as if we never existed when we are completely burned out or when we die by suicide."

There was a heavy silence in the room before Bailey added, "Wow, that was something. It's a toxic environment indeed, Nina. No wonder we have such high staff turnover. Self-care isn't a substitute for leaving a toxic job. Honestly, sometimes leaving is better than half staying. I'm very angry that nothing's been done yet to address the death of Dr. Hummingbird. Bringing in the chaplain and the music therapist hardly does it. No wonder most staff didn't show up at the debrief; people are angry, very angry. We hear there might be an all-staff debriefing event soon, admin is bringing some kind of speaker, an expert, but we're looking for concrete actions to address the root causes of why our people end up quitting or dying. This is a cycle that needs to be broken through institutional and systemic changes, permanent proactive solutions, not some empty words or knee-jerk changes of a few policies and procedures."

"I have a massive headache, and need to go home now," said Nina. "I need some alone time to process how I feel about all of this. I'll stop by Darlene's parents this evening to check if they need anything before the funeral. This is disgustingly surreal."

"Let them know we're thinking of them," one colleague said. "Please take care of yourself, Nina," said another. Staff were not sure how to show support to their grieving colleague or even how to feel about the whole situation.

To lose a colleague to suicide is an ugly experience, one that brings up strong and heavy emotions and deep existential issues like stigma, guilt, and self-doubt. Teams need to come together to grieve and heal after such tragedies. For Nina, this was the last straw. She had been thinking for a while about quitting. Darlene was one of the few reasons she had not done it yet.

Dr. Wible (2016) writes about high suicide rates among caregivers:

> According to Medscape, 400 physicians die by suicide in the USA every year. That is equal to a whole class of medical school. Yet no one seems to track that data. The system is more interested in

hiding the bodies. Putting it another way, one million Americans lose their doctor to suicide every year.

Imagine the airline industry's outrage if every year 400 people died in a plane crash for predictable reasons. Imagine how many more thousands of caregivers in other parts of the world are going through the painful experience of losing a colleague to suicide or ending their own lives.

Sometimes we lose a coworker to suicide. The silence then weighs heavily on our souls, and guilt and self-blame might get magnified. It is crucial here to try to do the following:

- Focus on the quality, not the quantity, of the relationship with the deceased, celebrating their life and not only mourning their death.
- Remember them without the added weight of guilt or anger. We have each tried our best, given the circumstances.
- Practice self-care. Losing a caregiver can crumble the foundation of the whole team. Remember that you can honor the memory of those who have passed by continuing their mission and, as appropriate, looking after their loved ones, especially the little ones left behind.

Burnout, according to Dr. Pam Wible (2016), is fatal:

- "The professional image we are forced to conform to is a prison." Many caregivers learn to push away their feelings, be flawless, and show no signs of "weakness."
- "Many have daily suicidal daydreams." It is therefore crucial we pay attention to the subtle changes in our coworkers

and listen when our colleagues and our loved ones give us feedback.

- "Not all suicide is by drugs. Many caregivers die by self-neglect." Many caregivers are workaholics and loners. We want to fix everything for everyone and do it right now. Emotional intelligence, however, is the ability to do the right thing, the right way, for the right reason, and at the right time. We need to do our best and then accept the outcome. We cannot do more than our best.
- "We should be very concerned about our colleagues who have lost the ability to cry." When emotions are numbed, it could be a sign of burnout. Colleagues who are shutting down and building walls need our attention, affection, and urgent intervention.
- "Let us create a world where no one has to write a suicide note."
- "Many caregivers spend their lives on the edge."
- Offering hope can be more healing than prescribing drugs.
- "Bring humanity back to the practice of medicine."
- "We need better understanding, more resources, and less stigma." That is how we could break the cycle for our heroes.
- "The instructions regarding suicide prevention are included in the suicide notes." We need to make things safe so people can talk, and then we need to learn how to deeply listen.

Systems can also help lessen the burden of suicide through interdisciplinary approaches, where administrators, practitioners, and the larger community closely cooperate and collaborate in the planning, coordination, and implementation of action plans to prevent or reduce the likelihood of future incidents.

A response to this silent pandemic takes the following into consideration:

- Pre-crisis planning. Systems that frontload and prioritize staff self-care at times of ease seem to recover more quickly at times of hardship.
- Staff from different disciplines like mental health and the chaplaincy are important members of the team.
- There needs to be coordination to keep the larger community updated and to control rumors.
- Available resources in the affected system and in the larger community need to be readily available and accessible to staff.
- Staff's self-care is vital.

Response needs to be respectful of the family's privacy and wishes when it comes to disclosing the cause of death and the funeral and memorial arrangements. What is important is to not treat death by suicide as a source of shame for the family or the team.

Other helpful tips:

- Emphasize the importance of grieving as a community.
- Do not force people to participate if they do not want to.
- Offer opportunities for individual and group support.
- Normalize grief, but do not romanticize death.
- Be careful with cultural and religious messages about the deceased being in a better place or about harshly criticizing or condemning the suicide act.

Other Systemic Symptoms of Burnout

Sleep disruption

Sleep deprivation risks countless lives. Dr. Wible (2016) describes it as "An advanced form of hazing, more thorough and relentless and of greater duration than any other hazing anywhere else." Both a cause and an effect of burnout, sleep disruption is both a key indicator and a primary cause of compassion fatigue. Imagine hearing an announcement from your airplane pilot just before take-off, or from your surgeon just before your operation, that they are sleep deprived: Would you trust them with your life? Fatigue clouds judgment and risks lives.

It is during deep sleep that much of the processing of traumatic memories occurs. When sleep is disrupted (for example when working a night shift or being on call overnight), the traumatic experiences never get processed and meaning-making does not take place. Over time, an accumulation of these unprocessed traumatic memories can lead to fatigue of the body, mind, heart, and soul. Bessel van der Kolk (2015) eloquently wrote about these impacts of trauma in his impressive book *The Body Keeps the Score*.

Self-medicating instead of seeking professional help

Dr. Wible (2016) writes, "Alcohol soothes without asking questions." Many caregivers use drugs to dull the mental anguish of the profession. "Non-punitive mental health care is almost impossible to find, yet liquor and alcohol are readily available without scrutiny or censorship," she continues, adding that "Many go underground when seeking help to avoid professional persecution."

Dr. Grace Chen, the primary care physician we met earlier, will find immediate relief in going to the bar after meeting with human resources about the critical lab value she overlooked. The system would do better by offering her and her daughter the support they need and deserve so that future errors are less likely to take place.

Barriers to reaching out

Sometimes there are resources and services available but staff are reluctant to use them. Some of the reasons behind that include

- lack of time,
- concerns about confidentiality,
- stigma, and
- limited access.

From Symptoms to Cures

Here are some ways to help dysfunctional systems become better able to support burned-out staff:

- *Create assistance programs.* Unfortunately, according to Wible (2016), many assistance programs act as both treating and policing agencies. Caregivers see them as having a serious conflict of interest. But mental suffering does not equal professional incompetence. These institutional bodies need to be infused with large doses of humanity and compassion.
- *Create a culture of expressing emotions.* In a culture that expects quick decisions, reflecting on personal troubles and difficult emotions becomes countercultural. Plight may then fall on deaf or unsympathetic ears. That causes mistrust of the system, and caregivers continue to "keep the secret" and remain stuck in a vicious cycle of silent suffering that can turn deadly. I have heard from many junior staff that they do not feel safe talking

about and processing witnessed trauma, because the system seems to shame and gaslight them for showing vulnerability. But is vulnerability not the ultimate sign of courage?

- *Build authentic relationships.* If you want to build trauma-informed systems, start with building authentic relationships. Almost every time I respond to a code that involves an agitated patient, I find that listening to them with compassion leads to de-escalation of the situation and a better outcome for all parties involved. We need to do the same with our caregiver colleagues; through building caring relationships.

Recognize emotional stress at the institutional as well as the personal level. A trauma-sensitive system is one that does not shy away from acknowledging the trauma story, that looks at its policies and procedures with a trauma-informed lens, and that offers opportunities for interested staff to receive trauma-focused training. Unfortunately, many times, caregivers who open up about these struggles face systems that tell them, "If we cannot see your wounds, they must exist only in your head." That message shuts down any future desire to reach out for help and adds to the culture of stigma and secrecy where those who are emotionally bleeding continue to walk wounded. These are very deep, very real, and very serious daily issues that need to be addressed. It is time that we start bringing the skeletons out of the closets.

Workplaces Function Within a Cultural System

For many, America is not the land of inclusion. In his impressive and heartwarming memoir *Call Me American*, Abdi Nor Iftin (2019) eloquently shines a bright light on the beauty of acceptance and diversity that America is proud of and best known for. But in this section I want to introduce the reader to a less known and rarely acknowledged aspect of these not very united states of ours. I know that discussions about hate are not easy and can bring up discomfort. My intention is not to dwell on negative messages and graphically detailed intricacies of hate or to ignite more fires, but rather to focus on the importance of not buying into the one-sided narrative and the divisive language of bigotry.

Some see this as a difficult topic to discuss. That is exactly why it needs honest conversations. Some have told me that the topic may be too much to digest and that bringing it up, especially these days, can stir up strong emotions. But who said that healing is supposed to be pleasant? I strongly believe that in order for our country and our world to heal, we need to have uncomfortable and difficult honest conversations, some of which, like this one, are quite overdue. I believe that hate is way out of style and that it is an ugly pandemic that needs to be eradicated.

I speak my truth, from my own perspective and I invite you to speak your truth and share your perspective. Every voice is valuable and every story matters. I have no intention to offend anyone, but I have no desire in downplaying or sugarcoating this malignant phenomenon. I will call hate out and call it exactly what it is.

A culture of hate is alive and well in many parts of this interesting nation, but it appears that the dark side of "America the beautiful" has been, for whatever reasons, a very well-kept secret, as many people seem genuinely oblivious to, and surprised by, the mere existence of the big invisible elephant of hate that might be residing next door.

People hate for many reasons, and sometimes they hate for no reason. Here are some of the reasons why people hate others, according to Allison Abrams (2017):

- ignorance, lack of exposure to different backgrounds (but is this really still acceptable in this time and age of social media and global villages?)
- fear of "the other," xenophobia, in-group/out-group mentality: "They're here to take over our country, jobs, resources, welfare system, etc."
- fear of oneself, commonly seen in bullies: "I'm not terrible, you are"
- lack of self-compassion: "What others do affects me"
- the need to fill a void (which is how deviant groups and dark ideologies attract and trap their recruits)
- societal, cultural, religious, and political factors, like misinterpreting a sacred text or quoting it out of context (but are we not supposed to see God's face in every face?)
- unresolved, transgenerational trauma

Hate Circuits, Cycles, and Impacts

The hate circuits

There are parts of the brain that are believed to be responsible for hate. These include subcubcortical structures like the insula and the putamen, and cortical structures like the frontal lobe. The neurobiology of emotions is a fascinating field that offers many opportunities for research that can help facilitate healing the deep wounds of hate.

The hate cycles

The longer and more frequently you are exposed to a hated or loved face, the more your brain is programmed and trained to respond accordingly. For example, some soldiers are shown faces of "the enemy" before deployment. This provides a golden opportunity for the fields of technology and psychology to collaborate and offer attractive alternatives to violence. We need to change the narrative by focusing on love instead. The bodies of our youth should not continue to feed the fires of bigotry. The role of caregivers is vital here: We cannot claim to be non-racists if we support systemic racism, and it is not enough to be non-racists; we should all strive to become anti-racists.

The impact of hate on the psyche and soul

Hate impacts self-esteem. "Your people are slower than molasses in January; I wouldn't expect you to know the answer; the likes of you will never amount to anything": These were the words a hateful teacher directed at my wife when she was the only child of color in her rural Colorado town. Even today, decades later, these ugly messages at times still haunt the child in her in the form of second-guessing herself.

Hate can lead to:

- doubting one's beauty and true potential,
- losing one's voice,
- trauma that sucks out joy,
- acting out what the "victim" does not have the words for,
- shutting down,
- lashing out,
- missing out on beauty, as traumatized children seem to grow older faster, and
- internalized racism.

I used to think, "Please, not another Muslim," every time I heard of a "terrorist attack." I no longer do that because I found my voice.

Now no one can speak for my religion or tell my story. I now own my narrative.

Justice Is Essential for Healing

Justice is an essential ingredient for healing. According to Dr. James Mason, here are 10 "easy" things you can do for justice:

- Do not laugh at racist jokes. Instead, interrupt. Do not let your silence speak for you.
- Make a conscious effort to get to really know people who are "different" from you.
- Learn about diverse cultures and traditions, show authentic curiosity, and be genuinely interested. This might entail getting out of your comfort zone and trying new things.
- Think before you speak and ask if you are not sure. Weigh your words before you utter them. Language matters.
- Be a role model. Be vocal in opposing discriminatory views and practices, and challenge unfair policies and procedures.
- Do not make assumptions. Examine your own prejudices and your explicit and implicit biases.
- Explore the unfamiliar. Firsthand exposure is enlightening and provides perspective.
- Work on projects with members of groups different from your own. Human connection helps heal the wounds of ignorance.
- Be a proactive parent. Expose your children to diversity and show them how to safely stand up for justice.
- Support anti-racist causes.

As a caregiver, you are invested in making the world a place of safety and beauty for everyone. Here are a few things you can try to that effect:

- Reach out to others, in service and in love. Check on people around you, get to know them, and make sure their needs are taken care of.
- Remember the less fortunate.
- Be grateful for the good parts of your life.
- Be mindful that in times of distress, many sources of comfort are denied. During the height of the 2020 global pandemic, even places of worship were forced to close, and since these usually serve as social avenues for communal gathering and leisure, people will hopefully show more attachment to and love for houses of worship. But also do not forget that God is found not only in these places; but you can see His beautiful face when you take care of people's needs and when you actively work on mending broken hearts, making sure that no one is forgotten or left behind. The best way to worship the Creator is to serve His creation.
- Focus on sharing, neighbors, and beauty. America has been deeply polarized during the recent past, with bad-mouthing and othering minorities becoming common. I can get angry and resentful, or I can commit to refusing to hate. Hate yields no results, so I choose love instead. I have been honored to write chapters in the books *Islamophobia and Psychiatry* and *Antisemitism and Psychiatry* and also to write about the struggles of youth recruited into militant groups in my book *Generation of ISIS: The Impact of War and Conflict on*

> We express in action our appreciation for all the caregivers in our lives, in our communities, in our country, and all over the world.

Children. I got involved in interfaith dialogue because what we have in common is much greater than what divides us, and because we have abundant beauty we could and should share with our neighbors and fellow citizens.

Discrimination in the Workplace

Hate crimes have increased in the recent past. According to the Federal Bureau of Investigation (FBI), more than 7,100 hate crimes were reported in 2017, a 17% increase from 2016. Most are motivated by bias toward race, ethnic background, religion, and sexual orientation. The FBI defines a hate crime as a "criminal offense against a person or property, motivated in whole or in part by an offender's bias against a race, religion, disability, sexual orientation, ethnicity, gender, or gender identity." Hate itself is not a crime, and the FBI is mindful of protecting freedom of speech and other civil liberties. Also, according to *Psychology Today* (Abrams, 2017), there are 917 organized hate groups in the country. Online hateful posts and comments have increased by 900% in the three years following the 2016 presidential election.

You should be able to recognize hate when you hear or see it. But even if you are in doubt, please prioritize safety. The choices you make and the stands you take matter. If it looks or walks or talks like hate, then it probably is.

Hate can surprise us in our workplaces. Hate sometimes follows us inside our very places of safety. In my mailbox at the hospital where I work, I once found a note that read, "America will be great again." I called my wife, who urged me to report the incident as a hate crime, but I went first through my supervisors. The nurse manager was deeply shaken. She kept sobbing while repeating, "I am very sorry, not here, this is not America, this is not who we are." We found out later that the note was written as a "show of support," by a staff member, but you can see how good intentions alone can backfire if the message is not clearly conveyed from the sender to the receiver. Most misunderstandings do indeed stem from miscommunication.

Caregivers who are people of color or who are "minorities" because of other demographics might face stress even on their days off work.

I recently drove through rural Oregon to enjoy the outdoors. My daughter and my sister-in-law wanted to use the restroom at a store, only to be told, "There are no bathrooms here for you. Allah is great," a phrase taken out of context and commonly used to ridicule Muslims and link Islam to terrorism. You can see how the ugly face of hate and the dark side of America can ruin your attempt to unwind after hard work serving people and saving lives. If you have never had to deal with a similar situation, be grateful, acknowledge your privilege, and show up for those who are "less fortunate."

In 2017, I attended a psychiatric conference in California and took my family to see Disneyland. When I went to join them later in the day, I found them very upset, as someone had insulted my wife. Somehow intimidated by the way she dressed, he said, "Those terrorists, they're everywhere, they don't belong here, they should go back to where they came from." Why would a real man utter those words of pure evil and lash out at a mother and her young children, who were just trying to have fun at a place that claims to be an international representation of joy? Trauma is ugly, and it can be found even in "the happiest place on earth."

It is quite taxing, mentally exhausting, and emotionally drain-

We may not know who around us is struggling with big feelings. You might never in a million years have the slightest idea what your fellow caregivers are going through when not at work. Always be kind. Everyone is fighting a hard battle.

ing to be on the receiving end of hateful statements like "You're not a true American," "You're not American enough," "You're not one of us," or "You don't share our values." And it is heartbreaking when bystanders remain silent while bearing witness to hate. Yet, I remain a firm believer in the goodness of humanity, and that it is love, not hate, that needs to be given more room in all our interpersonal spaces and our human interactions. We admire beauty because of the ugliness and we appreciate light because of the darkness. Similarly, we need to address hate safely, honestly, openly, authentically, and courageously before we can embody what love truly means. My mom always told me, "If you can't be the source of someone's joy and delight, don't be the source of their pain and distress." Leave people feeling better than when you came into their lives and make every interpersonal space safe.

Practice Cultural Humility and Self-Awareness

Cultural humility and engagement with "others," according to the Center for Adolescent Studies, means to be "other-oriented and aware of your own blind spots, to step outside your conditioned ego, to commit to self-reflection and self-critique, to work on fixing power imbalances, to develop partnerships with marginalized groups and people, and to advocate for system-level changes."

- Watch for microaggressions. There is nothing micro about aggression. We need to confront the covert and overt forms of aggression before they turn into transgression and eventually violence.
- Watch for your own contribution. If you are the
  - perpetrator: STOP (Stop, Take a deep breath, think of Options, and Pick the one with the best moral value). Appeal to your forebrain (logical/rational mind) to weigh your choices and examine your humanity and morality;

- bystander: ACT (Assess safety, Connect/cause a distraction, and Take a stand). Trust your midbrain (emotional mind) to detect the smoke and sound the alarm; or
- victim: RISE (Raise your voice/speak up, Involve, examine Safe options, and Exit with dignity). You might have to resort to your hindbrain (primitive/reptilian mind) to survive.

- Model interest in and curiosity about other cultures. Caregivers can play a vital role in combating hate through showing interest and curiosity in the different demographics of the people they care for, and healers who come from diverse backgrounds can do that by being proud of who they are and sharing their uniqueness. We should not feel the need to hide any aspect of our identity to fit in. I personally believe that if someone does not like something about me, then it is their issue, not mine.

It is important to emphasize that if the care we provide is not culturally sensitive, then it is not trauma informed. The same is true for us. We need to honor our cultural needs and cumulative trauma. Medicine is sometimes called the field of suffering. Trauma raises ethical dilemmas and stirs moral and existential problems deep within us. No wonder the wounds we sustain are considered moral rather than mental injuries.

On the day after the New Zealand Mosque shooting that led to the death of 51 worshippers in 2019, a Jewish neurologist called to introduce himself and check on me. He was willing to reach out and show up for a total stranger. His kind gesture made that horrific day a little less painful. Never underestimate kind gestures. A small act of kindness toward someone you do not know, or toward your fellow caregiver, can make all the difference.

- Support your colleagues when they speak up. Early one morning, I walked in on the night-shift staff at my hospital and heard the only staff person of color say, "The only reason the patient is in restraints is because he's Black." You could hear the dead silence in the room. No one spoke up. It was an awkward moment before people started to disperse. I am ashamed to admit that I, too, for some reason, did not speak up that day. Weeks later, I asked for everyone's attention and addressed that nurse, saying, "I wanted you to know that that morning I heard you loud and clear, and I am so sorry I didn't speak up right then and there." It is better to follow every rupture with a repair. I believe that doing the right thing, even if late, is better than never doing it.
- Pursue social justice. After going through many experiences of hate and bigotry, I joined multiple social justice causes in my community and started to work with organizations on ways to make the world a better place.

I am reminded here of the story of a Rabbi who marched with Martin Luther King on a Saturday, and when asked about worship and being with his congregation, he replied, "Today, my feet are doing the praying."

The main message of this book is to encourage breaking the cycle of silence. Speaking up is always the right thing to do, and it needs to be part of the culture of caregiving.

The Healing Power of Listening

My mentor, Professor Richard Mollica (2018), in his impressive manifesto, wrote:

> Healing practitioners listen, listen more, and listen again to all shades of trauma expressed in different forms, representing uncovered memories. Modern medicine not only has the right, but the moral obligation, to address human cruelty and violence as leading causes of illness and death. The shocking silence in our medical field is so loud, it is deafening.

Here are excerpts from Dr. Mollica's manifesto *Healing a Violent World* that you may appreciate:

- "The goal of healing is to relieve human suffering."
- "We declare that the patient is a beautiful living organism that freely acts and loves in a family and a community and is not an isolated body part or a disembodied mind. The healer must have a relationship with the human in their social and cultural context."
- "The healer will understand that humiliation is a major instrument of human violence that is systematically applied to others to annihilate the individual, their family, and society. Humiliation creates hopelessness, despair, anger, and revenge (often existing together) in the violated person. Humiliation must be acknowledged for its victim to be released from its tight grip."
- "Only through imagination can healing occur. The survivor and the therapist create within themselves the image of a whole and complete human being who has shed the pain and suffering of the illness state caused by human cruelty."

- "Except in beauty there is no healing. Beauty is the salve and ointment that creates our healing spaces and healing relationships. We will fight against all institutions and practices that are vulgar, ugly, sterile, and demoralizing. Beauty is healing's greatest ally."

Dignifying Mental Suffering

According to Mollica (2018):

> Social forces that can impair the psychiatric patient's efforts to normalize his/her life include:

- The dominant role of biological explanation for mental illness that orients psychiatric treatment; the emphasis on diagnosis without treatment goals; and the use of drugs without supporting therapies.
- Professional expectations that certain patients are resistant to treatment or incapable of benefiting from professional care.
- Bewilderment as to the central therapeutic role of the trauma story.

Healing the healer

Professor Mollica (2018) continues his manifesto by saying that "Everything in our world is calling for help, but few listen." Healing the healer, according to him, means that:

- Empathy comes at a cost. Little by little, healers accumulate the pain of others, therefore it is important to practice self-empathy through self-care.
- We decry the industrialization of modern medicine where

patients are transformed into consumers, and we revolt against the thousands of checkboxes that now define our patients.

- We are repulsed by the ugliness of many healing environments.

The Healing Power of Justice

Professor Mollica (2018) believes that there is no true healing without the focus on justice. His manifesto goes on to state:

- There is no healing without justice. Justice brings order and beauty.
- Injustice is a personal and social cancer. If it cannot be treated, it needs to be cut.
- Injustice makes us sick. Treating humans unfairly causes them physical and emotional distress.
- All humans have the right to a culturally effective healthcare.
- Storytelling to those interested in restoring justice can pull people out of isolation, shame, and humiliation.
- I will be acting in bad faith if I ignored the monumental task of ending human violence while my patients struggle to cope with atrocities of unspeakable horror.

But what can we realistically do as individual caregivers? I believe that, as a caregiver, we have lots to contribute to justice and healing. We do that if we

- try to reduce the aggression in our everyday life toward everyone around us,
- work on restoring human dignity with all our patients and coworkers, and
- engage beauty in everyone and everything around us.

> Be a "go-giver." According to Bob Burg and John Mann (2007), these are the five secrets of being a go-giver:
> - Your true worth is determined by how much more you give in value than you take in payment.
> - Your income is determined by how many people you serve and how well you serve them.
> - Your influence is determined by how abundantly you place other people's interests first.
> - The most valuable gift you can offer is yourself.
> - The key to effective giving is to be open to receiving.

The healthcare field can help tackle societal issues like poverty, violence, and racism. For caregivers, the human voice is sacred. Sometimes that means stepping outside of our comfort zone. "Stepping right into discomfort means stepping into the allies' zone. When we raise our collective voices, that is when we stop the hate," said Dr. Suzanne Barakat (2016) in her captivating TED Talk about the murder of three of her family members in North Carolina in 2015.

As a caregiver, here are things you can do about injustice:

- Advocate, through getting involved in causes.
- Connect with "others." Do it skillfully and respectfully. Do not act like a savior or take away their power. Trauma survivors need to be empowered, not enabled. Do not make them believe that they are broken or permanently damaged because of what happened to them.
- Use your "privilege." This could be your gender, age, race, legal

status, sexual orientation, position of authority, physical or mental ability, and so on, to speak on behalf of those who are oppressed and voiceless.

- Practice self-compassion, by being the best version of who you are.
- Community healing activities are vital in the aftermath of trauma. Build friendly structures and partnerships to encourage such programs.
- Keep the children out of this mess. Our children should not learn to hate others. Left alone, they will engage with other children regardless of background.
- Find the human connection. You do not have to be a therapist to be therapeutic. You do not even have to know the language or the culture to be helpful. People will appreciate you being humble and authentic. The language of humanity is universal. Humans have the power and capability to cause the most damage to each other, but also the most healing.

Cultural disparities can create "others" and a "not like us" type of mentality. Marginalizing people and forcing them to live on the edge of society can have disastrous consequences for their physical and emotional well-being.

Health is a holistic concept. Many factors contribute to illness and wellness. According to the Office of Disease Prevention and Health Promotion (ODPHP), examples of social determinants of health include:

- availability of resources to help meet daily needs
- access to educational, economic, and job opportunities
- access to healthcare services for all, because health, including mental health, is a basic human right

- quality of education and job training
- availability of community-based resources to support community living and provide opportunities for recreational and leisure activities
- social norms and attitudes (e.g., discrimination, racism, and distrust of government)
- exposure to crimes, violence, and social disorder
- socioeconomic conditions (e.g., concentrated poverty and the stressful conditions that accompany it)
- residential segregation
- language/literacy abilities
- access to mass media and emerging technologies (e.g., cell phones, the internet, and social media)
- culture

STAMINA stands for:
- S: Start early.
- T: Teach, through example.
- A: Assign tasks and responsibilities, toward self, family, community, society, and the world.
- M: Make it safe to express emotions.
- I: Interpersonal skills are vital relational tools.
- N: Network of healthy people and resources can function as a safety net. It takes a village to heal an individual.
- A: Allow room for growth through making mistakes. Learn that failure is a step closer to success. Never jeopardize your high ethics or lower your moral standards, but also make sure to be realistic and flexible. Reward the effort, not only the result; and celebrate the journey, not only the destination.

I believe in honoring justice as an integral part of healing. Going through the journey of forced displacement made me pay special attention to and learn as much as I could about asylum seekers and refugees so that one day I could use these tools to become a healer. My specialized training with the Harvard Program in Refugee Trauma was crucial in preparing me for the grave impact of human violence and the magnitude of global tragedies, and in giving me the passion and the tools to look for beauty along the way, even within those who hate my guts.

We can all contribute to recognizing and adapting to cultural differences we encounter. Just as, in the story presented earlier, Mr. Sinclair and Dr. Salam embarked on a voyage toward common healing grounds, we can do the same, through

- honest self-inventory, discovering and working on our conscious and unconscious bias;
- getting educated—we do not have to visit every country or speak every language to be culturally humble;
- refusing to hate, and actively working on embracing love;
- not sugarcoating the issue of hate or downplaying it but, rather, calling it exactly what it is;
- not placing the burden of fighting hate on the shoulders of its recipients; and
- speaking up and safely confronting all forms of aggression. Hate and violence do not happen in a vacuum. They happen because they are allowed to happen, and they will stop happening when they are no longer tolerated.

Stand up for justice:

- Refuse to hate and start with your loved ones. Rebuild trust, and repair broken bridges.
- Be a holding space for others.
- Provide space, offer grace, and respect pace of how people relate their stories and navigate their journeys.
- No one deserves to live on the margins of society. Sit with those who are otherwise forgotten.
- Make every interpersonal encounter a space of absolute safety and dignity.
- For some, we might be the only source of safety and sanity.
- Be a lighthouse, a beacon of hope, a dispenser of joy. You might be someone's last or only lifeline.
- Help people find, rather than lose, their beauty, and never kill anyone's spark.
- Of course, do not forget yourself when caring for others.
- During difficult times, let us focus on the beauty of our shared humanity.

Look past the labels, beneath the surface, and behind the curtain. Help people feel safe to unmask. You will likely find many pleasant surprises in "others."

In the next and final chapter, I want you to meet you. We have seen the pain and joy of being with clients and their loved ones, the pain and joy when our caregiving work impacts our families, the pain and joy of being part of the healthcare industry. Now I would love for you to explore not only the pain but also the joy of sitting intimately with yourself. This requires a generous amount of grace and self-compassion. Enter with reverence, awe, and love into the landscape of those who continue to provide healing despite their wounds.

Reflection Corner

Welcome to this sacred space. This is a breathing room. It is for you to pause and reflect in if you wish to do so.

Thank you for your courage.

You have seen the impact on your soul when working within systems and cultures.

Make sure that the pain imposed by rigid and bureaucratic systems does not take away from the joy of your caregiving.

I invite you to do something kind to your heart, like
- reach out to a social support network,
- join or build a community of care,
- make amends, and forgive others if you wanted to, and
- enjoy the beauty around you.

4 / The Caregiver Within

The Value of Introspection

In this section, I ask for grace as I share aspects of my own trauma story. I have been through multiple traumatic experiences but will talk here mainly about the encounters that led me to the caregiving field.

When I was 6, my 14-year-old sister suddenly went blind. An aggressive brain cancer had stolen her eyesight and, soon after, claimed her life. Seeing my father crying and my mother heartbroken ignited my passion to become a healer. I decided to pursue medicine, and even fantasized about becoming a brain surgeon, but every time I entered the operating room I ended up on the floor from fainting. I guess you cannot really be a good neurosurgeon if you are always unconscious.

At age 11, on my way home from school, I was almost kidnapped. In Libya in the 1980s, children did not know that humans can do ugly things to other humans, and parents did not warn their kids that some interactions with adults can be unsafe or even deadly. So when a man stopped his car claiming to be lost and proceeded to ask me for directions, I thought nothing of it. When I approached the car, I found him naked from the waist down, and as he attempted to grab me, I took off running and hid behind thick bushes until he finally gave up and drove away. That incident made me decide to work on trying to protect children from violence, especially that of a sexual nature. It is a sad world we live in that makes children fear adults who are supposed to be the very people entrusted to look after them.

I did extremely well in medical school and started working as an emergency room physician, but even then I was attracted to people's trauma stories and was looking for ways to tend to their emotional needs and mend their wounded hearts. I knew deep down that psychiatry was my passion, my true calling, and my cup of tea, but there was lots of stigma and cultural baggage attached to the field, so I worked as an ER physician until the age of 26, when I was forced into exile. My father knew through his connections that the government had placed my name on its "wanted" list because of my humanitarian activities. I had to immediately leave Libya, the country I deeply love, and was able to say goodbye to just Mom and Dad before boarding a boat and crossing the Mediterranean Sea to Europe.

Libya was a dangerous place at the time. I remember going to visit a friend who was recovering from oral surgery. When we parked in front of his house, four cars surrounded us; 16 masked men with all kinds of rifles and big guns were about to shoot at someone who was simply in the wrong place at the wrong time, a case of mistaken identity.

Going through the asylum-seeking journey was a humiliating experience. From the minute the boat landed in Malta, the immigration officers referred to the Libyan refugees as "dogs." I waited until I arrived in the United Kingdom before applying for asylum, but even in England I was called derogatory names, and my case for obtaining permanent residency was rejected. The immigration judge declared that "There was no evidence of physical torture" on my body, but what he failed to see were the scars of trauma on my mind and the deep wounds in my heart and soul. I was about to get deported back to Libya when, through a divine intervention, a friend introduced me to my future wife, a Libyan who grew up in Colorado, and that is how I found myself in the "Land of Opportunity."

Coming to a post-9/11, traumatized America as a young Arab Muslim man was another traumatizing experience. The country was bleeding, as its wounds were quite fresh after the terror attacks. I was called a "terrorist," and was told to "go back home," and was asked, "How's Osama?" and "Where's your camel?" People who had never met me before decided to judge me based on misperceived notions. Assumptions that are not only dangerous but also lethal to the body, the psyche, and the heart and soul of the one on the receiving end of hate and prejudice. This is what trauma does: It forces us to crawl into narrow corners, where we see "others" as enemies.

Even with my medical degree and wearing the white coat, I was still told by some people, "Don't blow up the hospital," and for a few years I was placed on the "no-fly list," was "randomly" selected for extra security screening whenever I went to the airport, and was even told by the dealership to return my car because "We don't deal with suspected terrorists." Fearmongering can indeed infuse hate into the fabric of the whole society.

I remember when security officers at the University of Colorado stormed the room where my wife was interviewing for a job. They told us that they had been "alerted that two suspicious individuals were in the building." We raised suspicion just because of how we chose to practice our religion and because we dressed differently. Ignorance makes us dismiss others. That is a shame. We miss out on beauty when we see only one side of the people we dismiss and when we decide that "others" are invisible.

In February of 2011, I left for my first mission to "free Libya" since my exile 12 years earlier. I was blessed to get connected with Medical

Teams International, a relief organization that donated nearly half a million dollars' worth of medical equipment to take with me. I drove the shipment from Egypt to hospitals on the frontlines of fighting. After returning to Benghazi, I found out that one of my brothers, a charismatic and well-spoken news anchor, was speaking against the new revolution. A group of angry youth surrounded my parents' home and threatened to set it on fire. They did not leave until they forced my youngest brother to publicly denounce his closest sibling.

The above encounters made me pursue further training in trauma mental health and disaster relief. Trauma can make or break a family. I have seen the damaging impacts of trauma on the family unit. It takes a special kind of family for family members not to see one another as enemies but rather face their trauma as a united front. The trauma my family endured was a driving force that set me on a mission to create Untangled, a model of care to break the cycles of dysfunction caused by trauma that can span generations. My hope and passion is to help mend broken hearts through bonding, empowering, and healing traumatized individuals, families, and communities, worldwide.

My traumatic grief and multiple losses at a young age are reasons behind my desire to serve. A child's smile is what brings beauty to our world, and when joy disappears from a child's life because of trauma, the whole world falls into darkness. My family came together to acknowledge and nurse our deep wounds, and I believe that is what added cohesion and brought some light to our home amid the dark tragedies.

With my specialized training with the Harvard Program in Refugee Trauma, I founded projects that focus on nonviolent conflict resolution, and on peacebuilding and reconciliation. I was aware that people tend to take sides in armed conflicts and that there are deep wounds on all sides. I conducted workshops in cities labeled as "pro-Gaddhafi" and took their invitation as a golden opportunity to build bridges and work on healing using civilized dialogue. That is what is needed after bloodshed and civil war. People need to sit down at the same table, humble their ego and respect and accept perceived differences, make compromises, try to meet in the middle, and unite in the process of grieving and healing. Grief is a communal affair, and regardless of their political affiliation, fighters should set aside their lust for revenge, for the sake of their country and for their children's future.

Trauma can visit you inside the safety of your bedroom. My wife and I try to make our home a safe space for our girls. We implement an open-door policy and remind our children that they can, and should, always feel safe to express their emotions and share their feelings with us. In one instance, at three in the morning, our oldest came knocking on our bedroom door to share a nightmare of receiving death threats. Hate is ugly. It terrorizes children's sleep and steals beautiful memories and precious moments from them. I wondered what might have happened if we had not had an open communication and safe connection with her. She would have most likely cried herself to sleep or found other unhealthy ways to cope with that terror.

Traumatized children grow older faster. The weekend after the mosque shooting in New Zealand, the weather was gorgeous here in Portland. My neighbors were enjoying a family barbecue, while I was meeting with other families brainstorming ways to keep our children safe when they walk into their schools and places of social gathering and houses of worship.

Sometimes you might feel the need to resort to dark humor as a defense mechanism to help you cope. When someone asked my wife, "Aren't you hot under that thing?" in reference to the hijab, her religious dress, she answered, "Oh, that's exactly why I'm wearing it," and when someone shouted at her, "Muhammad's dead," she shouted back, "Duh." I hope you can see the irony here. Dark humor is not really that funny, and hate takes a heavy toll on the soul.

Being of service is something that my parents instilled in me from a young age. My late mother visited the sick and families of the deceased every time she heard about them. Many times, these were total strangers. She told me, "I might not know the family, but I know they are in pain." Mending broken hearts is a sacred act, and it can happen in very subtle ways. Let us strive to make it our daily habit to brighten someone's day and lift their spirits.

But showing up for others might mean getting out of our comfort zones. When my wife finished her talk about Islam and interfaith dialogue at a local church, the women in attendance were deeply touched and asked if they could show solidarity through wearing the hijab for a day or protesting the travel ban. She asked them, "Would you take a bullet for me?" The room fell silent. Her point was that combating hate is not a one-time decision we make or a single stand we take, but rather a way of life and a daily active commitment. In the words of Shahina Siddiqui of the Islamic Social Services Association, "Tears are appreciated, and prayers are wonderful, but they do nothing to dismantle the systems and structures of hate."

I am a strong believer that humans are fundamentally good. I had many people extend a hand of support and solidarity at a time I needed that the most, for example my residency program director Dr. David Allen, who offered me a position at the University of Tennessee and supported my application for the Harvard trauma program. He even wrote a letter to immigration urging them to expedite the approval of my permanent residency so I could obtain my green card and fly to Egypt to visit my sick mother. He was a Jew who gave a Muslim a chance to realize his dreams.

This is just a taste of my trauma story. A small glimpse of what life might look like for caregivers who get treated differently because of the way they look, talk, or practice. Yet, these encounters made me more passionate about serving and renewed my commitment to refusing to hate. My trauma story is what transformed me into a healer. What about you? What was your inspiration to join this wounding, yet healing, industry?

Caregivers come to the field for many reasons, for example:

- personal or family experience with suffering
- personal or family experience with the healing power of caregiving
- desire to support people during difficult times
- caring about causes (like homelessness, mental illness, addiction, end of life, etc.)
- intrinsic rewards that come with being a healer
- In the words of a young nurse that I had the pleasure to interview:

I chose nursing to be close to the human experience, to walk with people on their journeys through the best and worst of times, to have deep existential conversations with them, to hear their stories of strength and vulnerability, and to bear witness to their pain and joy.

But caregiving can be a lonely experience as well:

- There may be no one to process feelings with.
- Caregivers might feel excluded from social circles.
- Other people, including our loved ones, might not understand what we do or what we go through, especially when caregiving brings mainly distress and heartache.
- Many caregivers are internalizers to start with. We think that emotions are for the weak.

- Many caregivers are doers and givers. We do not feel comfortable receiving or sitting still.
- We are held to high standards, and sometimes we are the ones holding ourselves there. We say things like, "Everybody comes to me. I don't recall the last time I said no. I don't delegate. I know that it'll be faster if I do the job, and I know that I'll do it better. I tend to be protective of my patients."
- We are fixers and cannot be "broken."
- We fear relational and professional repercussions for showing our human side.

But caregivers continue to care despite all the pain they endure while caring, for these reasons:

- It is rewarding and fulfilling work. "Any other job would leave me empty."
- Our patients appreciate us. "I might not remember all of my patients, but they'll remember my kindness."
- The good (the joy) overshadows the bad (the pain).
- We want to make a difference. "I want to care for people during the toughest times of their lives because I know what it's like to feel the ground crumbling beneath me."
- "Often our patients come to us on the worst days of their lives. To end up as a patient, especially with a serious physical or mental illness, your life might feel unmanageable and dark. I want to bring a little light to that moment."
- It is a higher calling.

One reason caregivers do not reach out to available sources of support is the ever-present worry about making mistakes, and the fear of malpractice. According to Jo Shapiro, when medical errors happen, we can support the caregiver if we

- reach out to them,
- listen to their side of the story,
- normalize the anxiety they experience,
- reframe what happened through humanizing caregiving,
- cope with what the caregiver might be facing, and
- encourage them to use available resources.

And according to *Stillpoint*, by Sheila Collins and Christine Gautreaux (2018):

- It matters what we say to ourselves.
- Do not organize your life around the convenience of others. Stop playing by other people's rules.
- Do not hurt yourself protecting others.
- Self-care should not be a burden or a taxing task. It does not have to only take energy, it makes energy.
- To become a dancer, one must dance. Similarly, self-care needs to be practiced with joy. When you perform self-care more often, you have less need for self-healing.
- Self-care is not "them vs. me," it is "them and me." It is rather the tuning-in to recognize early on the subtle signs of burnout. We do not have to hit rock bottom or get deathly sick to get well.
- If you focus on your stillpoint, you can dance at high speeds and experience ecstasy without getting dizzy.

Skills of self-care that the authors of *Stillpoint* encourage include these:

- sorting and separating what belongs to us from what belongs to others
- letting go and surrendering, and learning when to do so
- building and using partnership powers to get help from others
- stepping back to see the "big picture"
- exercising the choice of saying yes or no

Self-Care Is a Duty

Caregivers are viewed as invincible. But it is very hard to serve as someone's last resort when your own resources are depleted. Some caregivers are so burned-out, they need to recover before they can even enjoy their time off. Yet, like moths, we are so attracted to the flames of our field that we do not know how to keep a safe distance.

If we do not take mental breaks, we might end up having a mental breakdown.

Healthy self-care does not mean taking a small pause to recover from engaging in a cycle of overdoing, but noticing early signs so we can interrupt the cycle before the damage is irreversible. We need to learn to master the skills of empathizing with our own needs.

When we give and never receive, we might start to resent the people we care for. Self-care might mean keeping your distance and saving your energy. Part of protecting your sanity is asserting your boundaries.

Some of us do not know how to keep clear boundaries without erecting a wall. But our needs count too. We need to find the balance between what we need for our own nourishment in relationships and withdrawing when it is time to do so. There is a reason that people with addiction recite the Serenity Prayer: "God, grant me the serenity to accept the things I cannot change, the courage to change the things I can, and the wisdom to know the difference." Caregivers need sobriety, too, not only ugly wakeup calls. According to *Stillpoint*:

> The caregiver's dance of self-care and self-healing cannot be a solo. Caregivers perform a communal dance. The intricate dance of balancing your needs with the needs of others may receive little applause unless you carefully select your partners. And even if you find no partners or audience, keep dancing. (Collins & Gautreaux, 2018)

The environment we work in, both physical and emotional, matters. If your environment is making you sicker than those you serve, pay attention. Sometimes the most self-caring and self-healing thing to do is to find a new environment.

Many times, you are not the captain, but that does not mean you have to go down with the sinking ship. Rather, use your power to save yourself from drowning; find a lifeboat.

Tips for Self-Compassion

Elizabeth Gilbert encourages us to practice self-compassion when dealing with difficult emotions. Here are some of her words of advice:

Of loneliness, she says: "The hardest person to be with in this world is yourself. How can I endure my own company if not for compassion (showing kindness from self toward self)." She urges us not to view isolation as terrifying and run away from it but rather to walk toward it:

> And you might get enlightened. It should not be an existential crisis to be alone with yourself. Be curious and do not rush the experience that could potentially transform your life. Many times, the

experiences that have the potential to intimately transform us are the ones we run away from. Get comfortable walking with curiosity and open mind toward your difficult emotions and most painful memories.

Other tips she shares with us include these:

- You do not have to look at the sky for a sign from the divine; look within. Watch external stimuli, but do not bring the external world into your seclusion, for otherwise the world will bring you panic, fear, and a sense of urgency. That will affect your intuition and your ability to help others. Be a better steward of your own senses. Being at peace with yourself cultivates the tools you can use to connect better with others.
- Reframe your perception of the stressors around you. A quarantine becomes a retreat when you invite you to meet you.
- Be aware of empathic overload and empathic meltdown. Replace them with compassion so you do not have to suffer, too, which prevents you from serving. There is courage in witnessing someone else's pain without joining in and inhabiting it. You realize that your suffering is not their suffering and theirs is not yours.

> *Value who you are, believe deeply in your worth, and demand respect through leading by example. You are overworked and underpaid, many times unappreciated. You are not only a servant of your community but also its leader. Lead with grace and confidence, but also fight for everything you need.*

- Show up through service, within reason, and without guilt about the inability to do more. There is always more need than what you have the resources for. Do what you can, then take care of yourself.

Healthy Caregivers Are Better
Able to Help Others Heal

All caregivers are vital to their care teams. Physicians, nurse practitioners, physician assistants, nurses, therapists, social workers, dentists, pharmacists, technicians, EMTs, chaplains, physical therapists, occupational therapists, massage therapists, speech therapists, acupuncturists, chiropractors, naturopaths, healthcare receptionists, and all those serving the healthcare field in security, transport, laboratory settings, food and janitorial services, interpretive services, and more—these are all vital members of the care team, but they are also an essential part of their families and communities.

Healthy caregivers bring better healing. To expect caregivers to be functional in their places of work when they are dysfunctional outside them is incomprehensible. Healthcare workers who feel vulnerable might internalize that, detach from their feelings, and act in ways that in the long run hurt them, their loved ones, their clients, and the systems they work for. Recall that Tasha struggled before finding that balance, and once she did so, she was more emotionally available to care for Mrs. Wilson and the other nursing home residents. Healthy caregivers bring healing because they feel safe, valued, and respected. Dr. Johnson took a clear position on behalf of Dr. Salam, and that made the resident physician feel like a valued part of a team that she will always defend.

When that is not the case, staff might find no other option than to exit. Nina could not continue to work at a place where she had lost her best friend. She left the emergency room and the addiction field to embark on a new career as a staff wellness consultant.

The COVID crisis was a cruel but much-needed wake-up call for the caregiving field. Caregivers do not live in a vacuum or behind the walls of fortresses. They are part of their communities, and they are always on the frontlines of response, starting with their families and expanding to their neighborhoods, schools, community centers, and places of worship. The global pandemic uncovered a healthcare system that is scandalous, to put it mildly.

Psychoeducation, therefore, is particularly important in the aftermath of trauma. Survivors need to know that most of the symptoms they experience are normal responses to an abnormal situation. Tasha normalized mourning for Mrs. Wilson and gave the grieving widow healthy tips on how to remember loved ones who passed and how to celebrate their memory and honor their legacy. She did that because she cared about her client, but also because of her relationship with her own mother and siblings and her new focus on self-care.

The mental health consequences of trauma are more than just PTSD. And even though most people who survive traumatic events do usually recover completely, some will have a difficult time coping. Remember the moral distress and the deep soul ache associated with caregiving? These shadows tend to haunt caregivers and hurt them more than physical wounds do.

What can caregivers realistically do in response to incidents of great emotional magnitude? We can do a lot working with survivors, like modeling self-care and self-awareness, and spreading hope. Working with interpersonal violence and man-made trauma is something that caregivers do on a regular basis, and many of them seem to have the tools, confidence, and expertise to engage survivors in meaningful and effective interventions. Remember Dr. Grace Chen, who poured her heart into her work, cared for thousands of patients as their PCP, felt comfortable listening to their stories, and also respected her own limits and boundaries. Like many caregivers, her challenges were not clinical but bureaucratic. The negativity of the system and the possibility of getting reported to HR or the medical board are real bogeymen, but she chose not to practice defensive medicine, because, for her, medicine is the industry of love. Caregivers can also speak up and be active agents of change. Alex raised his voice and joined the hospital leadership team, where he would be better able to make the emergency room a much safer place to work for himself and for his coworkers.

With the global scare over the COVID-19 pandemic and similar large-scale natural and man-made disasters, caregivers have a unique opportunity to explore new territories and play vital roles in helping the general public cope and heal. I am encouraged to see many colleagues getting comfortable consulting for the news media about masks, vaccines, and also about issues like burnout and social justice causes.

Trauma comes at a heavy psychosocial price. The invisible wounds and mental scars of trauma can go unnoticed, leading to long-term dysfunctions and, at times, transgenerational transmission. The suffering might extend beyond classical "psychiatric" symptoms to include somatic, academic, vocational, and mainly relational and moral struggles.

Here is my plea to you. Caregivers who work with trauma survivors should show the utmost sensitivity and tenderness to their clients, and the most grace and compassion to themselves. With trauma survivors, "What happened to you?" is a better question than "What is wrong with you?"—especially when dealing with patients who come through the doors of the system over and over again. It is important to not only see the challenging behavior but to also bear witness to the pain. The same is true when caregivers are in pain.

Time to recovery after trauma varies, not only among communities as they try to rebuild, but also among families and individuals as they try to piece together what happened to them and make meaning out of their trauma stories. Recurrence of symptoms is possible at times of high stress; survivors therefore will be served well if educated and equipped in advance.

In the aftermath of trauma, it is vital for survivors to regain the sense of safety, established routine, structure, and a semi-normal state in order to feel that they are back in control. Examples of community response are the random acts of beauty and kindness shown to strangers, such as reaching out to someone sitting alone at a restaurant or checking on a total stranger crying in a corner of the airport. We all deserve to be tenderly held and tended to.

Please always reach for beauty and joy amid stories of pain. Stories of trauma can penetrate deeply to our very emotional core, but when we choose to practice beauty in our interpersonal spaces and our relationships, people start to see the hope for healing. When Dr. Salam listened to the pain of Mr. Sinclair, and when Arjun saw the sacred in Joy's final moments, new common grounds were founded. It is amazing how small acts of kindness can touch, mend, heal, and even change hearts.

Forming connections out of chaos and weaving disparate events into coherence can lead to making meaning and can bring people a little closer to finding closure. When the emergency room teams came together to defend nurse Tiffany when she was assaulted, and to celebrate the life of Dr. Hummingbird after her suicide, everybody started a journey of healing. There is power in human connection. According to the book *What Happened to You?* (Perry, 2021), "Connectedness has the power to counterbalance adversity."

It is important to express empathy but also to watch for vicarious trauma. Empathy is to feel the pain of others without owning it. Walking the walk for those we serve is both arrogant and demeaning, as it takes away their power and instead gives us the podium, where we start to insert our own narrative and unintentionally become part of the abusive system. The staff at the hospital looked with mercy after Joy, who was dying of endocarditis induced by intravenous drug use. In a way the staff became her family and made sure she was given a chance at a last connection with her loved ones. Their actions dignified her life and beautified her death.

Vicarious posttraumatic growth means that we both get transformed going through the journey. Brad, a Jewish physical therapist, found bonding with Dr. Salam, a Muslim resident physician. They both shared the trauma caused by experiencing hate but found grace and a holding space for its root causes.

Healing is a journey, a lifetime commitment, and you cannot pour into others from an empty cup. We are wounded, we might have cracks, but self-care ensures that we do not break. Grace was injured by the healthcare system that was interested in micromanaging and punishing her mistakes, was wounded by a society that looked at her with suspicion during the COVID-19 pandemic because she was Asian American, and was hurt most by the toll trauma had taken on her relationship with her daughter.

Invest in Beauty

I have made it a habit to look for beauty in everyone I come across, and I have been pleasantly surprised with how much beauty I have discovered. This is the case whether it is in the struggles of someone with mental illness, drug addiction, or homelessness; or in the stories of those living with dementia, developmental delay, or physical disabilities; or through visiting refugees, orphans, and the many others who go unnoticed and are usually forgotten.

It is true that not only in America but throughout the world, difficult conversations are taking place in many homes, including those of caregivers. Children are getting exposed at an early age to discussions of heavy topics like violence, hate, and human cruelty. Committing to building a safe home means having an open-door policy and encouraging our loved ones to share their tears and fears with us. I rather my children ask me the difficult questions they wrestle with.

We need to hold open spaces in our hearts for others. According to Richard Mollica (2018):

> You do not have to cross thresholds or borders to find yourself in others' stories. You find yourself in them and they live again in you, you are all of them and they are you. Unfortunately, with the industrialization of modern medicine, patients are becoming mute, and healers are becoming deaf. There is lots of silence in the therapeutic space.

Helping others heal helps heal healers. Wounded healers who seek to heal others are transformed in the process of healing. The ice that needs to melt is often within ourselves. The person in need is an agent of healing for the caregiver. Tasha needed to hold Mrs. Wilson's hand and with her mourn not only the beloved husband but also her own late brother Jerome and the new relationship she was building with her dementia-stricken mother.

The very act of caregiving is transformational, leading to the caregiver's personal and professional growth. Healthy caregivers provide better care.

When wounded healers heal, they become better able to care for others, and they can contribute more as productive members of their communities and the larger society.

Even though I had my "fair" share of trauma, I would never change a thing about my story. My experiences with trauma made me a better son, a better husband, a better father, a better physician, and most importantly, a better human.

I have many reasons to succumb to despair, buy into hate, or believe in divisive messages, but I choose beauty instead. I find plenty of beauty in you, and that is why I wrote this book in the middle of a global pandemic. I write because you are my inspiration and because your story is worth narrating and sharing.

Now What?

What a journey this has been, full of heartache and soul pain, but also full of beauty and joy.

You are the foundation of thousands who are standing on your shoulders. If the foundation weakens, then the whole structure will collapse. Self-care is therefore not a luxury; it is a responsibility.

When my sister-in-law was recently deployed by her hospital to another state and was required to work in a COVID unit, she did not know what she was signing up for. The hospital was overwhelmed. I knew that she would be coming back home with compassion fatigue, if not total burnout. The "orientation" the staff received about the impacts of trauma was minimal, as expected. It went something like this: "You're about to jump into rough waters. Make sure you don't go to the deep end. Good luck, now jump." She is an empath and returned home heavily wounded, having had to watch many patients die without their loved ones around, and having to bear witness to staff breaking down because they are human. We are humans, not machines, and we will reach a point where we snap. Our PTSD is industry-induced, an occupational hazard, a heavy price we pay for caring, a moral injury. She was able to find some healing by leaning on her faith and family, and she is back at work despite her fresh wounds because she wants to continue to care, and because, like me, you, and other caregivers, the field holds that power over us, the power of love. I recently lost my uncle and his wife to COVID-19. They died six hours apart. He was too young to die and was too far away for me to look at him one last time, in the eye, and say how much I miss and love him. If your loved ones are around, cherish them.

Caregiving is like being in a war zone. Even in armed conflict, fighting parties declare a cease-fire and take a time-out to rest. Make sure you do so as well. We continue to find joy despite the horror when we invest in taking care of our needs first and foremost.

Now what? What is next? This is not a goodbye; far from it. I would like now to extend an invitation, asking you to write the next chapter of this book, or write your own book, through deepening your kindness toward your clients, your family, and your community, but most importantly through being extra kind to yourself.

Deep kindness and compassion are virtues that are worth sharing, and most of the time they get reciprocated many times over. Most people are like pure gold; humans are sacred creatures, precious treasures, so if we keep digging, we will discover hidden beauty. We need to invest in, and commit to, unconditional humility, acceptance, and love, and we need to imagine, and work toward, a world where we celebrate what we truly have in common, rather than fight over our perceived differences. A world that practices deep kindness is a place I long to live in.

Reflection Corner

Welcome to this sacred space. This is a breathing room. It is for you to pause and reflect in if you wish to do so.

Thank you for being you.

You have seen the impact of caregiving on your body, mind, heart, and soul. Make sure that you nurse your wounds and tend to your pain so you can continue to have joy in caregiving.

I invite you to do something kind to your soul, such as
- pray (if prayer is part of your spiritual practice),
- narrate your story,
- practice gratitude, and
- engage in acts of grace.

Thank you for your service, for your commitment, for your courage, and, mostly, thank you for being you.

Conclusion

This has been a deeply humbling and an extremely emotional journey for me. I hope you had joy reading a book written about you. Please tend to your soul, be extra kind to your heart, and engage in plenty of self-care activities.

It has been my absolute pleasure, honor, and privilege to write a book with you, for you, and about you.

You are my hero and inspiration. You might be wounded, yet you continue to be a healer.

We continue to heal others despite our bleeding wounds because that is who we are; we are wounded healers.

Afterword

I t is my hope that you, the reader, upon reflecting on Dr. Reda's book *The Wounded Healer*, will come away with a deeper understanding of the mystery of woundedness in each of your lives. Ancients of years past and we seekers of today have tried to understand and find meaning in the untoward experiences of daily life. They, and we, have discovered we have limitations, shared human boundaries, and common imperfections and woundedness. In a culture that values perfection at all costs, it is hard to admit we are not perfect and indeed we have wounds that cry out for healing. What is within a person who, after experiencing profound suffering, turns to forgiveness and compassion rather than self-hurt? This in a word, is the message of Dr. Reda's book.

Our greatest challenge as healers is allowing Soul to speak to us where we meet, like Adam and God reaching out in Michelangelo's Sistine Chapel painting. It is here one meets a Compassionate and Merciful God. Imperfection does not mean we are not good enough or that we are tainted by woundedness. Imperfection implies that we, as caregivers, have areas of growth and healing.

My reaction to Dr. Reda's work is one of a shared journey as a wounded healer. I found myself lost in reverie as my own insights emerged about my path. It takes a great amount of humility to make known to the world one's vulnerability. It takes a great amount of courage to offer one's journey of healing as an opportunity for the reader to experience hope and a renewed sense of the gift of being a caregiver. Dr. Reda does this with skill and soul, interweaving his professional skills as a psychiatrist with his heartfelt faith in the human spirit graced by the Divine. He knows how to witness to wounded healers because he is one.

In his own journey of overcoming trauma, Dr. Reda discovered his calling as a caregiver in the practice of psychiatry, specializing in trauma. Working with clients and staff in the healthcare setting, with immigrants living where he practiced, and taking trips to refugee camps and war zones to work with children, he continued to reflect on his experiences. He felt the tension of choosing compassion over violence. He chose the path of compassion. He knew the pain of trauma; he had experienced it as he endured much suffering in his homeland and after being forced to leave it. He knew the pain of being an immigrant in a strange land that was both welcoming and suspect of immigrants of the Islamic faith. He knew the pain of being marginalized, which prompted him to be more engaged in the service of others.

The Soul of Caregiving, A Caregiver's Guide to Healing and Transformation, was the vehicle that brought us together. Soul resonated with him that created a bond of brotherhood. We come from different faith traditions; Omar, a devout Muslim, and I, a practicing Catholic. We were born in different countries and cultures; I, born in New Jersey, USA, and Omar, born in Libya. Today, Omar lives with his family in Portland, Oregon, and I live with my partner in Atascadero, California. He, a trained psychiatrist with special training from Harvard; I, a Doctor of Depth Psychology and a life coach, author, and speaker. And yet, we met and share a common vision of brotherhood, and a deep understanding of Soul. I am honored to share this unique brotherhood with Omar.

Thank you for being a wounded healer sharing your wisdom to those who feel overwhelmed with pain and suffering. You offer a Divine light that leads to healing and transformation.

Edward M. Smink
Author of *The Soul of Caregiving: A Caregiver's Guide to Healing and Transformation*
September 2021

References

Abrams, A. (2017, March 9). The psychology of hate: Why do we hate? *Psychology Today*. https://www.psychologytoday.com/us/blog/nurturing-self-compassion/201703/the-psychology-hate

Barakat, S. (2016, November 7). *Islamophobia killed my brother. Let's end the hate* [Video]. TED Conferences. https://www.ted.com/talks/suzanne_barakat_islamophobia_killed_my_brother_let_s_end_the_hate?language=en

Burg, B., & Mann, J. D. (2007). *The go-giver: A little story about a powerful business idea*. Portfolio Books.

Center for Adolescent Studies. https://centerforadolescentstudies.com

Cherry, K. (n.d.). *Biography of psychologist John Bowlby*. Verywell Mind. https://www.verywellmind.com/john-bowlby-biography-1907-1990-2795514

Collins, S. K., & Gautreaux, C. (2018). *Stillpoint: A self-care playbook for caregivers to find ease, and time to breathe, and reclaim joy* (2nd ed.). Earth Springs Press.

Federal Bureau of Investigation. (n.d.). *What we investigate: Civil rights: Hate crimes*. https://www.fbi.gov/investigate/civil-rights/hate-crimes

Figley, C. R. (Ed.) (2012). *Encyclopedia of trauma: An interdisciplinary guide* (1st ed.). SAGE Publications.

Figley, C. R. (Ed.) (1995). *Compassion fatigue: Coping with secondary traumatic stress disorder in those who treat the traumatized* (1st ed). Routledge.

Gilbert, E. (2020, April 5). *It's OK to feel overwhelmed. Here's what to do next* [Video]. https://www.youtube.com/watch?v=oNBvC25bxQU

Himelstein, S., & Gonzalez, M. (n.d.). Center for Adolescent Studies. https://centerforadolescentstudies.com

Hollifield, M. War Survivors Institute. https://warsurvivors.org

Iftin, A. N. (2019). *Call me American: A memoir.* Vintage.

Kraft, H. (2020). *Deep kindness: A revolutionary guide for the way we think, talk, and act in kindness.* Tiller Press.

Krasuski, J. The American Physician Institute for Advanced Professional Studies. https://www.americanphysician.com/

Mason, J. L. http://jameslmasonphd.com/

Mitchell, J. International Critical Incident Stress Foundation. https://icisf.org/mitchell-phd-cts-jeffrey-t/

Mollica, R. F. (2018). *A manifesto: Healing a violent world.* Solis Press.

Moreland Capuia, A. https://www.dralishamorelandcapuia.com/

Perry, B. D., & Winfrey, O. (2021). *What happened to you: Conversations on trauma, resilience, and healing* (1st ed.). Flatiron Books.

Reda, O. A. (2019). *Untangled: A go-to guide for caregivers of traumatized children, families, and communities.* Chehalem Press.

Robinson, B. E. (n.d.). *Author bio.* https://bryanrobinsonbooks.com/bio/

Schimmel, A. (2021, June 8). Rūmī. Encyclopedia Britannica. https://www.britannica.com/biography/Rumi

Shapiro, J. (n.d.). *Jo Shapiro, MD, senior consultant.* https://safeandreliablecare.com/jo-shapiro

Siddiqui, S. Islamic Social Services Association. https://www.issacanada.com/

Smink, E. M. (2018). *The soul of caregiving: A caregiver's guide to healing and transformation* (1st ed.). Wise Media Group.

van der Kolk, B. (2015). *The body keeps the score: Brain, mind, and body in the healing of trauma.* Penguin Books.

Wible, P. (2016). *Physician suicide letters—answered* (1st ed.). Pamela Wible, MD.

Wood, S. (2012, January 21). *Compassion fatigue: Caring for the caregiver* [Power-Point slides]. https://www.slideserve.com/Olivia/compassion-fatigue-caring-for-the-caregiver

Index

beauty (*continued*)
  caregivers in finding, 22–23
  invest in, 175–77
behavior(s)
  as only the message, 17
  problem, 17–18
belief(s)
  false, 45
bonding
  with children, 77–83
bottled-up emotion
  expression of, 31–32
boundary(ies)
  asserting healthy, 3
  in protecting caregivers, 15–20, 27
  respecting one's, xxiii
"Breaking Through," 85–87
broken systems
  dismantling, 125–38. *see also under*
    burnout; traumatizing systems
Burg, B., 152
burnout, xviii
  American Physician Institute on, 126
  assistance programs for dealing with,
    137
  barriers to reaching out, 137
  build authentic relationships in
    avoiding, 138
  in caregivers' healing, 47–51
  create culture of expressing emotions
    related to, 137–38
  described, 47
  false beliefs and, 45
  family impact of, 83
  as fatal, 133–34
  fight against, xxvi–xxvii
  MBI on, 47
  professional help for, 61–62
  self-medicating vs. seeking
    professional help related to,
    136–37

sleep disruption related to, 136
soul ache related to, 6
suicide related to, 127–35. *see also*
  suicide
symptoms of, 136–38
workplace systems contributing to,
  126–27

Call Me American, 138–39
caregiver(s), 159–79. *see also under*
  caregiver within; caregiving
  bearing witness to stories of, xxviii–
    xxx
  boundaries protecting, 15–20, 27
  Center for Adolescent Studies
    guidelines for, 27–28
  challenges facing, xxiii–xxiv
  checking in on, 9
  in finding closure, 22–23
  during COVID-19 pandemic, 71,
    171–73, 177
  emotions showed by, 8
  families essential for, 69–74. *see also*
    under family(ies)
  feeling tangled, xxiii
  in finding forgiveness, 22–23
  healing of, 28–62. *see also specific*
    types and caregivers' healing
  healthy, 171–78
  as hosts, 5–6
  "Hurt People, Hurt People," 10–15
  in finding meaning, 22–23
  neglect of own needs by, 2
  price for being, 6, 7
  priorities for, 52
  putting own needs last, 29
  reasons for becoming, 165–67
  respecting one's boundaries, xxiii
  roles of, 16, 22–23
  self-awareness of, 2–3, 27–28
  self-care by, 2–5, 121–23

children (*continued*)
  healing of, 93–103
  individualization needs of, 101
  self-determination needs of, 101
  of trauma, 93–100. *see also* children
    of trauma
children of trauma, 93–100
  be anchor for, 100
  be there for, 96–97
  described, 93–95
  help child live his/her childhood,
    95–96
  identities of, 97–99
  know window of tolerance for stress,
    99–100
  model unconditional love for, 100–3
  parental absence impact on, 97
  parents distancing themselves from,
    96–97
chronic stress
  acute stress vs., 39
CISM network. *see* Critical Incident
    Stress Management (CISM)
    network
client(s)
  pain and joy of interacting with,
    1–63
closure
  caregivers in finding, 22–23
Collins, S. K., 167–69
communication
  authentic, 27
community healing activities
  injustice-related, 153
compassion
  fatigue in flattening, 3–4
  in PTSD management, 41
  self-. *see* self-compassion
compassion fatigue, xviii. *see also*
    caregiver fatigue
  in caregivers' healing, 45–47

compassion resilience as byproduct
    of, 3
  coping with, 9
  false beliefs and, 45
  HALTS related to, 53
  institutional measures and attitudes
    in mitigating, 123
  PTSD vs., 46
  reasons for, 62
  stages of, 46
  steps to avoid, 48
  symptoms of, 47
  vicarious trauma vs., 48
Compassion Fatigue, 7, 123
compassion resilience
  as byproduct of compassion fatigue, 3
connection
  in dealing with injustice, 152–53
cooperation
  family-related, 81–83
cortisol, 39
countertransference
  described, 16
courage
  of wounded healer, xvii
COVID-19 pandemic
  caregivers' roles during, 71, 171–73,
    177
crime(s)
  hate, 144
Critical Incident Stress Management
    (CISM) network, 123–24
cultural humility
  in workplace, 146–48
cultural system(s)
  workplaces functioning within, 138–
    57. *see also* workplace
culture(s)
  of care, 9–15, 125–38
  of expressing emotions, 137–38
  of hate, 139–42

in healing within healthcare industry, 117–24

curiosity
  witnessing individuals in distress and, 19

Daughter-Father Bonding (DFB) project, 80
Daughter-Father Bonding (DFB) YouTube channel, 94
death
  coping with, 51–59
deep kindness
  described, 93
Deep Kindness, 93
DFB. *see* Daughter-Father Bonding (DFB)
difficulty(ies)
  humor in navigating, 17
discrimination
  in workplace, 144–46
disorganized family attachment style, 79
distress
  bearing witness to individuals in, 19–20
DNA imprints
  of unacknowledged trauma story, 40
dysfunctional systems
  dismantling, 125–38. *see also under* burnout; traumatizing systems

emotion(s)
  bottled-up, 31–32
  caregiving impact on, xxii
  expressing of, 8, 137–38
emotional stress, 125–38. *see also under* burnout; traumatizing systems
empathic meditation, 36, 42
empathy
  self-, 36
  of wounded healer, xix

Encyclopedia of Trauma, xxv, 122
enlightenment
  trauma-related, xxvii
environment
  toxic, 118–21
eye contact
  in healing, 108

false beliefs
  compassion fatigue and burnout related to, 45
family(ies)
  "Abandoned," 64–68
  appreciation in, 72–73
  attachment styles of, 78–80
  bonding with children, 77–83
  "Breaking Through," 85–87
  burnout impact on, 83
  caregiver fatigue impact on, 64–83
  caregivers', 69–74
  cooperation within, 81–83
  healing power of, 64–115
  listening by, 72–73
  partner appreciation in, 74–77
  quality time in healing within, 109–10
  reflection corner, 115
  refueling tools for, 73–74
  resilience within, 77
  self-awareness in, 72
  self-care in, 71–72
  trauma impact on, 64–68, 83–88. *see also* traumatized family
family attachment styles, 78–80
  how to improve, 80
family–work balance
  in healing, 103–6
fatigue
  caregiver. *see* caregiver fatigue
  compassion. *see* compassion fatigue
  compassion flattened by, 3–4

FBI. *see* Federal Bureau of Investigation (FBI)
Federal Bureau of Investigation (FBI)
  on hate crimes, 144
feeling(s)
  suppressed, 30–32
Figley, C.R., 7, 117, 123
forgiveness
  caregivers in finding, 22–23

Gautreaux, C., 167–69
Generation of ISIS: The Impact of War and Conflict on Children, 143–44
Gilbert, E., 169–70
go-giver(s), 152
grace
  in combating stress, 22
gratitude
  through caregiving, 16

HALTS (hungry, angry, lonely, tired, scared), 53
  compassion fatigue and, 53
Harvard Program in Refugee Trauma, xv, xix, 59, 155, 162, 164
  on mindful meditation, 36
hate, 139–42
  culture of, 139–42
  cycles of, 140–41
  impact of, 141–42
  reasons for, 139–40
  in workplace, 139–42, 144–46
hate circuits, 140
hate crime(s)
  defined, 144
  FBI on, 144
  prevalence of, 144
  Psychology Today on, 144
healer(s)
  healing of, 150–51
  warrior, 21–23
  wounded. *see* wounded healer

healing
  caregivers', 22–23, 28–62. *see also* caregivers' healing
  caregivers in, 171–78
  of children, 93–103
  doing what matters most in, 88–91
  factors in helping, 102–3
  family in, 64–115. *see also under* family(ies)
  of healers, 150–51
  within healthcare industry, 117–24
  helping others in, 176
  House of Joy in, 107–11
  as journey, 175
  justice in, 142–44, 151–57
  listening in, 149–50
  professional assistance in, 103
  quality time in, 109–10
  reflection corner, 115
  of relational wounds, 92
  This Is Us, Together in, 112–14
  trauma responses in, 91–93
  work–family balance in, 103–6
healing activities
  community-related, 153
Healing a Violent World, 149–50
health
  as holistic concept, 153–54
  ODPHP on social determinants of, 153–54
  whole, 59–60
healthcare industry
  assaults within, 118–20
  caring systems within, 123–24
  dismantling traumatizing systems within, 125–38
  healing within, 117–24
  leaving vs. staying, 120–21
  sexism within, 120
  tend to your soul, 121–23
healthy lifestyle
  components of, 49–50

Mann, J. D., 152
Maslach Burnout Inventory (MBI)
    on burnout, 47
Mason, J. L., 142
MBI. *see* Maslach Burnout Inventory
    (MBI)
meaning
    caregivers in finding, 22–23
Medical Teams International,
    161–62
medicine
    described, xxvi
meditation
    empathic, 36, 42
    mindful, 35–37
    patience through, 42
    in self-care, 35–37
mental scars
    trauma-related, 173
mental suffering
    in workplace, 150–51
microaggression(s)
    in workplace, 146
mindful meditation
    Harvard Program in Refugee Trauma
        on, 36
    in self-care, 35–37
mindfulness
    Center for Adolescent Studies on,
        76
    described, 36
Mitchell, J., 123–24
Mollica, R. F., xv–xix, 36, 42, 60–61,
    149–51, 176
Moreland-Capuia, A., 92

NGOs. *see* nongovernmental
    organizations (NGOs)
nongovernmental organizations
    (NGOs)
    approaches of, 125

ODPHP. *see* Office of Disease
    Prevention and Health Promotion
    (ODPHP)
Office of Disease Prevention and Health
    Promotion (ODPHP)
    on social determinants of health,
        153–54

pace
    in combating stress, 22
pain
    sharing, 40–42
parent(s)
    absence of, 97
    of children of trauma, 93–103. *see*
        also under children of trauma
    distancing themselves from their
        children, 96–97
    needs of, 89–91
    refueling tools for, 73–74
    resilience of, 77
    self-care by, 77
partner(s)
    appreciation for, 74–77
patience
    through meditation, 42
patient–caregiver relationship. *see*
    caregiver–patient relationship
Perry, B. D., 37, 91
Physician Suicide Letters–Answered, 127–28
play-therapy techniques, 76
posttraumatic growth
    vicarious, 175
post-traumatic stress disorder (PTSD)
    compassion fatigue vs., 46
    management of, 41
"privilege"
    in dealing with injustice, 152–53
problem behavior(s)
    case example, 17–18
    as only the message, 17

About the Author

Omar Reda is a board-certified psychiatrist, a Harvard-trained trauma expert, an author, and a family advocate, but most importantly a dreamer, and a strong believer in the potential of finding beauty in all human encounters—even those heavily impacted by trauma.

This book is an attempt to honor caregivers and help them find the joy of caregiving.